THE BROTHER YOU CHOOSE

THE BROTHER YOU CHOOSE

PAUL COATES AND EDDIE CONWAY TALK ABOUT LIFE, POLITICS, AND THE REVOLUTION

SUSIE DAY

AFTERWORD BY TA-NEHISI COATES

THORNDIKE PRESS
A part of Gale, a Cengage Company

LIBRARY OF CONGRESS CIP DATA ON FILE.
CATALOGUING IN PUBLICATION FOR THIS BOOK
IS AVAILABLE FROM THE LIBRARY OF CONGRESS.

ISBN-13: 978-1-4328-8497-0 (hardcover alk. paper)

Published in 2021 by arrangement with Haymarket Books

Printed in Mexico
Print Number: 01   Print Year: 2021

CONTENTS

PREFACE:
LIFE, POLITICS,
THE REVOLUTION

This book is about Paul Coates and Eddie Conway, who met years ago, neither can remember exactly where or when, in the Baltimore chapter of the Black Panther Party for Self-Defense (BPP). Eddie and Paul are two solid, intelligent, funny — two very different African American men, who, through time, space, and all their differences, remain connected. This book is about their lives, their politics, and their friendship. Just that simple. Just that complicated.

In 1970, Eddie Conway, twenty-four years old and Lieutenant of Security for the Baltimore BPP, found himself facing charges — based on sparse, governmentally skewed evidence — of fatally shooting a police officer and attempting to kill two others. Scores of local people pitched in to help Eddie, including Paul Coates, who knew Eddie slightly, but didn't much like him. Although this support probably allowed Eddie to escape the death penalty, he was given a sentence of life plus thirty years. Finally, in 2014, on the strength of a recent legal precedent, Eddie Conway was released from prison.

All during the years that Eddie lived behind bars, Paul never left him. Now that Eddie's out, Paul's still around. Today, Paul is the celebrated founder of Black Classic Press, one of the few remaining independent publishers of work by and about people of African descent. Paul is also the father of seven children. Over the decades, as he built his business and raised his family, Paul visited Eddie in prisons all over the state of Maryland, often taking his kids — one of whom is the writer Ta-Nehisi Coates — with him.

I too visit friends in prison and have done so for more than twenty years. Most of these people come from a protest lineage that crested in the United States when a new Black militancy was emerging from the civil rights movement. These were years when the Black Panther Party for Self-Defense formed around a Ten Point Program beginning with the revolutionary imperative that Black people determine their own destiny; when Indigenous Americans fought to take back what little remained of theirs at places like Wounded Knee; and when many white people sidetracked their life trajectories to end racism and the Vietnam War.

The people I visit are serving life sentences or the equivalent. They're convicted of breaking the law — sometimes using armed struggle — in their fight against imperialism or racism or patriarchy or capitalism. They see their cases as part of the fight for The Revolution. Back in their day, The Revolution was something many people fully believed was just around the corner.

Some of these people living long years inside actually did what they were charged with. Others have been framed by law enforcement, set up. Eddie Conway is one such person.

I first met Eddie in 2012 when he was in his forty-second year of incarceration and well into his sixties. With my partner, Laura Whitehorn, I visited him at the Jessup Correctional Institution, just outside Baltimore. The Jessup visiting room was bleak and fluorescently lit, with the usual din of conversations from other visits going on. Yet, even amid all the standardized grimness, it was actually fun talking with Eddie.

Hearty and personable, with a keen sense of humor, Eddie got into talking, among other things, about the sci-fi books he loved, especially the *Star Trek* series. He struck me as a deeply ethical person, interested in and informed about the politics of the day. I wasn't surprised by any of this: among the disproportionate numbers of Black and Brown people inside its prisons, the United States holds some of the world's most enlightened and morally diligent human beings.

What did surprise me, though, was Eddie's absolute certainty — given his forty-plus years into a life-plus sentence — that he was soon to get out. Laura and I saw Eddie in September; he told us he expected to be home with his family by Thanksgiving.

A Black Panther convicted of killing a cop? Yeah, right.

To understand how farfetched Eddie's idea of getting out seemed, look back into history and see how intolerable the reality of the Black Panther Party was to the United States government. After the assassination of radical Muslim leader Malcolm X in February 1965; after the Watts Rebellion six months later, when residents of a Black Los Angeles neighborhood, fed up with police brutality, destroyed over 40 million dollars' worth of property; after almost a hundred

10

years of Jim Crow laws and the lynchings and police killings of unarmed African Americans that accompanied them, the Black Panther Party for Self-Defense emerged rather quietly in Oakland, California, in the fall of 1966.

The civil rights movement, by the mid-1960s, had, according to some accounts, basically played itself out.[1] In seeking a legal end to racial segregation, using dignified public pressure and respectful, nonviolent protest, the movement achieved phenomenal victories. But the passing of the Civil Rights Act in 1964 and the Voting Rights Act in 1965 did almost nothing to address the daily poverty and discrimination endured by most Black people in the United States. Then suddenly, the Panthers appeared as a force demanding answers beyond the reach of established laws.

Twenty years earlier, the United Nations had issued a Declaration of Human Rights proclaiming the equality and freedom of every human on the planet. And, with the Soviet Union and the People's Republic of China providing support to independence movements in Africa, Asia, and Latin America there was, for the first time, the hope of a global uprising that would liberate colonized and subjugated peoples. The Panthers saw themselves as part of this movement for socialist revolution — and not only for Black people.

The Panther program evolved to demand liberation for all people of color and all oppressed peoples around the world. Inspired by the Cuban revolution, Algerian independence, anti-colonial resistance in Vietnam, Panthers studied the Marxist-Leninism that helped structure revolutionary movements outside the United States. They read — and sold — Mao Zedong's *Little Red Book* (*Quotations from Chairman Mao Zedong*).

The political charisma of Huey Newton and Bobby Seale, who started the Panther Party in Oakland, galvanized the public. Chapters sprang up around the country as the Black Panthers began addressing everyday realities of Black life that the civil rights movement could not.

Panthers monitored and tracked beat cops and were occasionally able to prevent police brutality by showing up, armed, during arrests of Black men and women. They promoted Black self-sufficiency with action plans such as the Free Breakfast for Children Program. On May 2, 1967, the Panthers grabbed international headlines when thirty Party members in uniform — tough leather jackets, black pants, black berets —

appeared at the Sacramento Courthouse, openly (and legally) displaying shotguns and rifles as proof that when they said "self-defense," they meant it.

The defiance of the Panther Party was deeply shocking to the ruling powers of the United States — the country with the largest stake in crushing a worldwide revolution. To law enforcement agents such as the FBI's J. Edgar Hoover, the rise of the Panthers portended the reappearance of the rage of Watts, newly organized and in freshly menacing form. The government became bent on infiltrating and destroying every chapter in the country, most notably through the FBI's Counterintelligence Program (COINTELPRO).

Today, in conventional mid-American classrooms and most news media, the Panthers are considered, if they're considered at all, as a macho mistake that destroyed the racial inclusion of the civil rights movement. Virtually none of the hope, the creative energy, the solidarity of the radical Black movement has remained in the collective consciousness of America's mainstream. But the lives and daily work of people like Eddie Conway, whom COINTELPRO effectively sent off to die in prison, illuminate who the Panthers were and what a vision of Black self-determination can look like.

Eddie's getting-out-by-Thanksgiving dream could not have stayed so strong without William Paul Coates. While Eddie was in prison, Paul Coates founded Black Classic Press, bringing to light the texts of Black scholars and historians, forgotten or gone unnoticed over generations. He did that, in part, to help Eddie in prison. Paul also cultivated a rich family life, working hard to raise his seven children and keep them safe from the police.

I met Paul Coates in New York sometime in the 1990s, probably at some leftist literary conference. For years, we'd run into each other at various book events. We didn't know each other well, but I always perked up at seeing him. When I visited Eddie at Jessup, I started learning about his connection with Paul.

Back in the late 1960s, Paul had a steady union job as a baggage handler for United Airlines, which was helping him start a family. He remembers:

It was the best job I ever had, because I got to read. I read newspapers from the West Coast, the *San Francisco Chronicle*,

He read about the Bay Area Panthers and got interested in the national Panther Party.

Paul began to hang out around the Baltimore Panther office as a community worker in the fall of 1969. There, he met Eddie Conway. The main thing Paul recollects about Eddie was his off-putting political correctness:

Eddie was this senior Panther. He really, really had his head up in the air somewhere. He had this reverence around him. Yeah, I thought he was an arrogant ass.

What seemed like arrogance to Paul might have been a suppressed state of alarm, as Eddie was beginning to suspect that the Panther chapter he'd assumed was a bulwark against racist injustice had been heavily infiltrated — maybe even started — by law enforcement agents. Eddie remembers:

There was barricades 24/7. Real barricades. We were under surveillance, and that's a stressful way to live day after day . . .

It wasn't until 1976 that the US Senate Church Committee revealed the extent of the problem. The reason for those barricades was largely COINTELPRO — designed to derail those social movements deemed by FBI director J. Edgar Hoover and his ilk as being "un-American." Although right-wing outfits like the Ku Klux Klan were nominally targeted for "neutralization," the brunt of COINTELPRO hit progressive movements, bearing down on antiwar and liberation groups, especially if the people demanding liberation were Indigenous, Latinx, or African American. COINTELPRO hit no group harder than the Black Panther Party, considered by Hoover to be "America's greatest threat."

Back in Baltimore, 1970, when Eddie Conway was arrested, Paul Coates began to see something in Eddie beyond the "senior Panther":

Something happened that gave me a different Eddie Conway. He showed me something that never changed. He was always on the side of people. He was true to those principles we swore to in the Black Panther Party. He was always, always straight with me. That straightness showed me a person I could be committed to. It was inside that commitment that our relationship grew.

16

During the years Eddie was in prison, he and Paul worked together on any number of projects, from legal campaigns, to political rallies, to books. Eddie remembers:

Paul was just there for whatever we needed. The Black Classic Press that exists today grew out of the fact that we needed to get political books to prisoners.

As it turned out, Eddie didn't go home for Thanksgiving in 2012 or 2013. Time passed and I assumed that Eddie's "out-by-Thanksgiving" had probably been something he needed to hang onto so he could last a little longer inside. Then early in 2014, Eddie's lawyer, Bob Boyle, phoned and told Laura and me to come to Baltimore for a court hearing. Keep it quiet because that hearing might get Eddie out.

It did.

That hearing wasn't The Revolution; it was more a case of justice working in mysterious ways. Based on a precedent-setting ruling called the Unger decision in the state of Maryland and some good lawyering, Eddie Conway was taken, on March 4, 2014, from Jessup prison to a downtown Baltimore courthouse. There, after a requisite amount of legal argument, the judge announced that Eddie was free to go.

Minutes later, Laura and I were standing on the sidewalk outside the courthouse. About five feet away in the biting March air, I saw Paul Coates locked inside the world's hardest hug with Eddie Conway.

There's a photo of that hug. I might have taken it; I can't remember. In it, Paul's grasping a cell phone he'd been using to snap pictures of Eddie in a jacket someone had just given him — his first civilian coat in forty-four years. There are more photos I do remember taking at a party a couple of hours later. Paul is showing Eddie how his cell phone works. Eddie — exhausted and placidly stunned by these wondrous gadgets he had heard about but never until now touched — is just smiling and smiling into his friend, Paul Coates.

Who are Paul and Eddie to each other? Is the word "friend" enough? Aren't they also comrades? Brothers? Paul and Eddie use all these words, though none completely works. Each man, after all, is not the primary person in the other's life. There are wives and children and colleagues and hundreds of other friends. "For us," says Paul,

it was always a matter of me and Eddie and then the world. You can see that if

18

you understand the Panther Party has never left me. If someone comes up to me and says, "I heard you were in the Panthers," Eddie's going to be present. Yeah, he's always, always there.

Both Eddie and Paul grew up relatively poor, without access to a lot of formal education. The kind of education they did have, they were often happy to skip out on. As the Vietnam War was heating up, each young man went into the US Army, and there each faced off against different, though comparable, hurdles. Eddie and Paul deeply wanted — want — not just racial equality, but a chance for Black people to shape a new world.

When they met, Paul and Eddie were in their twenties. They are moving now through their seventies. Paul has dedicated his life to the written words of Black people, chronicling and commemorating the many thousands gone. Eddie, inside prison, counseled, mentored, and organized Black communities. Outside prison, he continues this work, besides covering prison issues for The Real News.

Paul and Eddie's story is one among many. It's unusual because it's ending well: people like Eddie — Black, convicted of murder — don't often get out. Other people, former Panthers as well as nonpolitical prisoners, remain inside more years, in worse conditions, without family or friends. Many die there. That's partly why seeing Paul and Eddie together and out in the world made me want to honor them with this book. I want to show this business-as-usual country, which daily disappears countless anonymous lives, how sometimes faithfulness and defiance can bring people back.

I want to let Paul and Eddie do the talking. They can't be understood outside of their own individual stories, told in their own inimitable voices. Or outside of their conversations that spontaneously combust whenever they get together.

A couple of months after Eddie's release, I began recording Paul and Eddie talking, separately and together, usually at Paul's office at Black Classic Press or Eddie's office at The Real News.

I asked them about their lives and politics. I've recorded hours of their talk, and from the texts I've transcribed, I've taken out maybe 64 percent of the references to Paul and Eddie laughing. These guys just yuck it up too much for my editing skills to handle.

I must add that my partner, Laura, who herself spent over fourteen years in prison on "un-American" charges, is a silent, though immensely welcome presence in this book. At the time of Laura's arrest in Baltimore in 1985, she had heard of a Panther named Eddie Conway who was doing hard time. Over the years, Eddie also heard of her, so their bond is deep. Laura sat in during many conversations between Paul and Eddie — who opened up about their feelings and politics in ways they probably wouldn't have without her there.

I wish there could be nuanced plot twists in this book, deft foreshadowing, startling character revelations. But the artistic stuff of novels wouldn't be very truthful here. I wish this book could deliver the full account of Panther life in Baltimore; Eddie's life in prison; Paul's life outside. But because this is just Eddie and Paul talking, many people and their related, equally worthy stories don't appear here.

I also wish I had had enough space and time to interview the formidable dozens of people like Cheryl Waters, Ta-Nehisi's mother, and Dominque Stevenson, Eddie's partner — and many of the women who've made up much of Paul's and Eddie's lives — who've led amazing lives of their own. But this story is enough: Eddie goes to prison; Paul sticks by him; Eddie gets out;

Paul and Eddie are still tight.

But that's where the beauty is. In this story lie galaxies of others, as yet unheard. Each person who has spent years in prison; each person outside, who has stood by someone inside, holds a story deserving volumes. But for now, because of real-life limitations, this is one small book about Eddie Conway and Paul Coates, talking about life, politics, and, of course, The Revolution.

■ ■ ■ ■

PART I

■ ■ ■ ■

Each generation must, out of relative obscurity, discover its mission, fulfill it, or betray it.
— Frantz Fanon,
The Wretched of the Earth

Part I

CHAPTER 1
HOW DID WE MEET?

Conversations between Eddie Conway and Paul Coates, recorded from real-life interviews, are formatted throughout this book a little like scripts for stage plays, with bracketed references to occasional laughter, significant physical gestures, etc. When necessary, there's a short introduction in italics — like this one — to set the scene. This conversation took place a few weeks after Eddie's release, in a room at Black Classic Press. Here, Paul and Eddie discuss the murky beginnings of their friendship.

EDDIE: Paul, how did we meet? You're mentally sharper than I am.

PAUL: Well, that may be true, but I really don't remember. It probably would have been at Panther headquarters.

EDDIE: What we started doing together was

probably going out to the airport and picking up Panther Party newspapers. Because there was a delivery problem; the newspapers were getting lost and misplaced.

PAUL: The government was "losing and misplacing" them.

EDDIE: It wasn't accidental. So we were trying to resolve those problems to get the newspapers on the streets every week.

PAUL: Since I'm so magnetic, he may have seen a friendship forming. You can tell how rough this guy is. [*Laughter*]

Of course, Eddie was more experienced in the Party. He was a Panther; I was at best a community worker. As I recall, I came to the Party, must've been the fall of '69. I would do breakfast programs and like that. Eddie wasn't somebody who came and went in a day. I recognized him as a Panther. But I didn't particularly like him.

EDDIE: Probably at the time I was the Lieutenant of Security.

PAUL: People came and went so much that the titles were kind of meaningless.

EDDIE: Sort of like, you're the Lieutenant of Communications because you already make the phone calls, you write the articles or deal with the PR. That made you a "Lieutenant" in that area. Me and Paul used to hang out before I got locked up. But I was his senior at the time.

PAUL: Yeah, Eddie was this senior Panther. He had senior-Panther-itis. Like, "I'm a *Panther.* You just came on the scene? Get out of my way, squirt." I thought he had an attitude about him, you know. I mean, I would spend more time with the Panther chapter than he did, but then Eddie would just pop up and *he* was the Panther. That largely came from the fact that he had been there so long. He was big stuff.

EDDIE: I don't think I was big stuff. Unlike Paul, I was kind of quiet.

PAUL: When I got to the Panthers, the Panther Party was closed. Even though those guys gave me an application to fill out. [*Laughing*] I never will forget it. I filled it out, but the ranks of the Panther Party had been closed in what, '68?

EDDIE: Yeah. After they closed the ranks,

27

the central headquarters in Oakland allowed Panther Party apparatuses to develop in certain areas. At some point, they even stopped that, and then some people started a group called the National Committee to Combat Fascism. In the midst of a flood of government attacks, headquarters didn't want more people to say they were Panthers.

PAUL: However, people did become Panthers largely through their practice. George Jackson said in *Blood in My Eye*, "You don't join us, we join you." So if people were acceptable, they were pulled in. But technically, from Oakland, they closed that stuff down.

This is actually how I became a Panther. I didn't join. It was after the defense captain, John Clark, who was in charge of the Baltimore chapter, was arrested, and Eddie and them all were in jail. I was still a community worker. So I went to New York to report to the leadership there and they basically said, "OK, John is gone. That means you're in charge."

I said, "I can't be in charge, I'm not a Panther." And they said, "Well, you're a motherfucking Panther *now.*" That was it. It wasn't a case of joining.

EDDIE: I was just thinking about where all this came from. I was thinking how lucky Paul was and how lucky I was. In most cases, people who were Panthers were living under the gun, so to speak, in those Panther pads, or in the Panther offices.

There was barricades 24/7, you know. Real barricades. We were under surveillance, and that's a stressful way to live day after day. You just couldn't put your work papers away in your briefcase and get in the car and go home.

CHAPTER 2
MARSHALL EDWARD CONWAY
— LOOK, THEY GOT
OUR STUFF

Long before they lived "under the gun," Eddie
and Paul grew up in separate East Coast cities, Eddie in Baltimore; Paul in Philadelphia.
They were both born just after the Second
World War, when liberation movements in
what was becoming known as the Third World
were taking on new life, and the 1948 United
Nations' Universal Declaration of Human
Rights became the first internationally agreed-
upon document to affirm the unequivocal
equality and freedom of all people, regardless
of race, creed, religion, or where they lived on
planet Earth.

But this awakening consciousness, which
would become the cornerstone of groups like
the Panthers, was still mostly unheard of in
Baltimore, when, on April 23, 1946, Marshall
Edward Conway was born to Eleanor and
Cleophis Conway.

Baltimore has traditionally been known as a
working-class city, a "melting pot," blending

Northern with Southern American cultural traditions. Factories, shipyards, and the people who worked in them over the years made possible today's upscale suburbs that exist in virtual isolation from the boarded-up row houses and poverty in neighborhoods like Sandtown-Winchester, now in danger of being "rescued" by gentrification.

Eddie started life in Cherry Hill, a mostly Black district skirting Baltimore's city limits. Today, it's considered one of Baltimore's "worst" neighborhoods. Back in the 1940s, it was a thriving Black working-class neighborhood.

Look, They Got Our Stuff

EDDIE: I was raised in a three-generation household in Cherry Hill. Myself and my sister were one generation; my mom, my aunt, my dad, and my uncle and then my grandmother and grandfather. We were all in the house. My grandfather was a stevedore. He would go down to the Maryland dry dock and unload the ships, so he might come home with a load of bananas or a sack with a huge turtle jumping around in it. My grandmother would cook, so the house would always be smelling nice.

Later, we brought my great-grandmother back. She had been living in Virginia on a family farm there and got too old to take care of herself. Then we had four generations. What I remember was a lot of running space and grass. It was really happy years for me, young, enjoying, just exploring and seeing stuff.

My dad was one of these Harley Davidson guys with the leather jacket and the bandana. Dad would ride his motorcycle, him and his little mob. They used to scare and terrify me. Dad would put me on the motorcycle and do 300 mph. My sister was laughing and happy, but I was just terrified.

My mom and my grandma were domestics. My mom was smart and quiet and she did the motherly things like seeing that we was secure and fed. My dad had been in the Navy during the Second World War, then he worked for the city. I'm not real sure what he did, but he had a government job, which probably resulted from his military service. I think that was the best he saw to do.

One of my aunts owned a beauty shop and she was a nurse. She was the one with ambition. But I don't know that my parents had any dreams or aspirations for themselves. On the weekends, they would all set around and drink beer and talk and get high and laugh and joke. But they didn't have a "skill set," I don't think.

At some point we moved into West Baltimore, where I started school. I remember that it was cold, but there was always candy and goodies. The classrooms had little wood- or coal-burning stoves. Pot-bellied things you couldn't get near. We had those in our house. I can remember us needing to heat up water in the big tubs to take baths.

This was the late '40s, early '50s. The neighborhood was really happy, bustling. We were right off Pennsylvania Avenue, in the heart of the Black community. Businesses up and down; big market, some of it open air, five-and-dimes, bars. The sort of thing you would see if you went up to 125th Street in Harlem fifty years ago. Cousins were around the corner, so we had friends to play with.

We would run around the neighborhood with the other children and watch TV. We'd go up on Pennsylvania Avenue and look in the stores and occasionally buy candy. Back then if you had five cents, you might be able to get a big [*stretches his arms out, wide*], BIG bag of candy like that. That was pretty much all we did. Of course, we went to school. Kindergarten for me, and first grade for my sister.

By the time I went to the third grade

[Public School #32], we had moved to a better house. You could say we were integrating the white neighborhood. There was a horse stable out back. It was fun; we could play and watch the horses. But in that year was one of the first things that impacted me.

I'm thinking I'm in the third grade; I can't be but maybe eight or nine. We did a Christmas play. We practiced and we learned and we're making the costumes, for maybe six months. You know, I'm not even sure I was in the play. Maybe I was the Christmas tree? No, it was probably a nativity play. Anyhow, when it was time to perform it, the school invited all our families, and then they realized they didn't have enough space to have it in our school.

So they bused us over to a white elementary school to put it on. And in my little mind, it was inexpressibly amazing. I thought it was like Harvard or Yale or something. There's a vast hall, there's the science lab, there's Bunsen burners and stuff.

Of course, we were completely out of control. We were little Black children and we had never seen any of this stuff — a science lab, a swimming pool. There's a track out around the school. So we go in the auditorium and we did the play. I don't remember anything about the performance itself. The auditorium and the play didn't even matter.

I came back from the play devastated. This was my first exposure to the white community. I didn't know. I never knew. Everyone I had seen — the doctor, the teacher, the butcher, the candlestick maker — was Black. Of course, I seen white people and storeowners passing through, but I had never been in their environment. This place rocked us off our foundation. We realized that in our little school we had been reading their old, used schoolbooks. We hadn't seen that these books had been hand-me-downs from World War II. This was stuff they had throwed away somewhere, and then they give it down to the Black school.

All of our books had written in them things like, "This book belong to Jim"; "This book belong to Betty." By the time we got a book, maybe ten people had owned it. In the white school we saw all these new books and encyclopedias and the swimming pool, the track. We realized we could have tucked our whole school into the side of that auditorium. I think we were feeling less than inferior — we were probably feeling like we were nothing. To think, here's your world: you're pumping water and you've got coal stoves — and then suddenly you go three miles away and there's running water and electricity and electric stoves and all the things you saw on TV.

Before, when we was looking at TV and seeing *Rin-Tin-Tin* or *The Lone Ranger* or *Ozzie and Harriet,* it wasn't real to us, it was just shows — because we knew what the real world was, or thought we did. The real impact was that it made us angry. But being little children, we weren't conscious of being angry. What we understood was, "Look, they got stuff. And look, we have nothing."

This is weird — I think I was so damaged that I don't even remember my fourth grade. I just didn't have a relationship with my school anymore. Us kids came back after Christmas and failed, academically. I just went — *FFFFT* — berserk. There was no bringing me back. I didn't know I was failing; I didn't care. I felt so diminished. And we started hooking school. All I remember about the next year was running up and down the railroad tracks with my little buddies.

The only thing that saved me, if I could call it that, was that the city took our house with eminent domain. They was going to build a police station on top of our house and we had to move.

So we relocated to East Baltimore, just when they were integrating. We were one of the few Black families that moved in, so the schools were good, and I got back into it. I did OK. But we knew the white people were running away.

In fact, one of my bad experiences — and it's a wonder I can still love white people — is my dog. Oh, the whole time, I never told you this. I had a little collie, like Lassie, only it was black, with a white collar, you know. Because my mom was a domestic worker is how I come to have a collie. The people my mom worked for had a collie that had a litter, and the family gave me one of the pups. He was called a blue collie because he was black and white. I raised this dog, and he was like a little pony for me. His name was Laddie. Laddie Boy. Oh, I'm so sad.

That family my mother worked for must've named him, too, because I don't think I would have ever named him Laddie! [*Laughs*] But he came with the name already. He was little. And we were also little when he came.

Well, after we moved over to the integrated East Baltimore neighborhood, the people up across the alley on the corner had a blond and white collie. They wanted to mate their collie with our collie, and my dad said, No, we're not studding him.

My collie used to run around in the house and the backyard. One day, he was gone. But we had just moved there, we'd been there for maybe three weeks. So we assumed that he got lost and couldn't find his way back. Meanwhile, the people across the alley had moved, but we didn't make the connection.

About a week later, Laddie came back. Raggedy. I mean he had traveled, apparently. We still thought he'd gotten lost, wandering around and then finding his way back, so we didn't put any extra protection on him. A couple of days later, he disappears again. But this time the neighbors across from us told us they'd seen the white couple get him. They came and they stole my dog.

We never seen him anymore. They never brought him back and we don't know where they went. But the neighbors seen them take him, so that's how we know he was stolen. And it hurt me. I was just really hurt about that. I didn't see it as a racial thing, I just thought they were stealing. But that always festered with me. They stole my damn dog.

I don't know what my parents thought

about it — this was big people's stuff. Maybe they just considered themselves lucky to be in an integrated neighborhood. All I know is, he was gone.

Black Rage, Undefined

EDDIE: When I started going to the more integrated school, it was an adventure. I was still angry but didn't know it. The reason I know I was angry now, after so many decades — we were twelve, thirteen — was that we would go and take the toys and the baseballs and ball gloves from white kids.

When we moved in, people were fleeing — white flight. We would go down to the neighborhood where the white people hadn't fled yet, and take their stuff. Or the white kids would come through our neighborhood on the bus from some magnet school like the Polytechnical Institute and we would snatch their radios. We would take stuff from them while they were setting on the bus. I feel bad about this now.

They were setting on the bus with their little portable transistor radios. Meanwhile, our radios were four-feet wide at home and plugged in. You can't be out on the corner with that. So we would snatch their radios. We never beat them up. I'm thankful for that. Most of the time we would just go and take their stuff and run off, and they would run the other way.

Of course, we wouldn't do this within a four- or five-block radius, because our parents would have had a fit if they knew. Miss Hattie would call your mother, you know? My folks just thought the neighborhood was great. The whites were moving out; we were moving in. The housing stock was still good.

But we knew we were poor because you could go four doors down where a white person lived and there's bottles of milk delivered every day, bottles of orange juice, chocolate milk, boxes of doughnuts. Of course, we didn't take any of that stuff; we would go to the next block or the block after. We were real little criminals, but it was criminals about stuff that we didn't get.

We did the same with the supermarkets. The pie truck would pull up and unload fifteen boxes of pies and doughnuts — just drop them off and leave them outside and we would go take them. We had a clubhouse in some garages set together, and we would take stuff in there and have little parties.

Now, it was all guys who would go out on these little excursions. The girls would never go outside the community and do things like that. They would be on the front steps or over at their girlfriends' houses. All of us were really very nice children, but there was an anger there, a Black rage that was undefined. There was no conscious effort to hurt anybody, but it was our way of staying, "This is our stuff." We never considered ourselves doing this in the aftermath of slavery. We just knew in some way that they had our stuff, and it was all right to take it back.

When I was little, I was never asked, "What you want to be?" I've never experienced that kind of interest in my future. That was missing and I never even knew it. You know, it may have been part of why we wanted things from the white kids, although the only kind of encounters we had with them boiled down to, "Give me that baseball glove." We might not have consciously known that the kid we took it from was supposed to grow up to be a surgeon.

Then I end up in junior high school, a wild and woolly place, beset with hormones. In fact, I failed eighth grade because I was beset with hormones. There was always some group hooking school.

I had no dreams then. No aspirations or picture of what I wanted to be in the world. Or maybe I did have dreams without realizing it. I started off drawing — I liked to

41

draw landscapes. And I had this thing about music. I started learning the piano, before I got distracted by the piano teacher. Distracted in the worst way — or best way. In any case, I didn't learn the piano.

But that's a really important question. What do you want to do in your life? There was no dreams, no hopes, no aspirations, no "You can be a doctor." My parents didn't set anything. Just, "Go to school, go to church."

Howard and Me: "Let's Get a Place, Then!"

EDDIE: Probably from the summer in 1959, when I was thirteen, I was Arabin'. Arabin' is having a horse and wagon with the food on the back and the fish or the whatever to sell. Every summer I would do that. My cousins would rent the wagon, and get a whole wagonful of stuff, and we would go down the street yelling, "Watermelons! Get your — whatever — here!"

I would be up on the wagon, guiding the horse and stopping him when it's necessary. We ran all over with the horse and wagon, into different neighborhoods selling the food, so I got to see a lot of the city.

By then I wasn't shocked by people's differences, so my life was quiet. I would hang

42

out with the guys, and because everybody knew everybody, it was a peaceful life, enjoying those teen, pre-teenage years. You had the occasional fight, but you also had neighborhood dances. Everybody would come together and party. So for about three years, I lived like that, enjoyed stuff.

When I was about sixteen, I somehow got this impression that I was grown. My job had changed from Arabin' to working at a car wash. I was bringing in a paycheck every week, and I thought, "Now I can buy stuff." So I told my mom, "I'm doing OK working this job. At the end of the summer, I'm not going back to school."

Of course, Mom did what moms do: "You can't live here if you're not going to school."

I'm like, "Not a problem. I got money."

I didn't realize that I had money because she was paying rent, electricity, food, water, clothes. So I had money until I moved, then the money was gone and I got to work harder.

Howard Reed, a buddy of mine, and I talked each other into moving into a house together: "Let's get a place, then!" One of our older friends signed for it. People were coming over and they'd party, stay up to two or three o'clock in the morning. But I had to go to bed at eleven o'clock, because

I got to get up at 5:30 and get my ride to work. So, five days a week I'm working and all my partying is gone.

I had no sense of direction and no motivation. The reason I think that's important now is because that's exactly the lack I'm seeing in Gilmor Homes with young people. The Gilmor Homes is where Freddie Gray grew up at. He got beaten to death there.[1] I'm now part of this network, "Coalition of Friends." Prisoners who get released start work there with Dominque Stevenson — professional people. We've been working there for a couple of years.

You can look into little children's eyes and see nothing. No hope, no future. Just vacant, "My cousin got locked up last week and my aunt may get locked up next week." Today, in most cases, the innocence is gone — and the hypocrisy is real. America says, "It's wrong and illegal to kill." But every time America wants something from people around the world, they go kill them and take it. Young people see this. In prison, that's what they used to tell me. "America wanted oil? They went over, they killed people, and they took it." They see the hypocrisy of "all men are created equal." It sounds good, but the reality?

■ ■ ■ ■

Back in my day, we were unaware we were innocent of the world. Rarely did we travel far from the neighborhood. Segregation didn't allow us for long in the bigger world. But we were never without hope. We thought that we would be OK. "We're children now, we're going to grow up and we're going to make it," you know? Make it as what? That thought never occurred.

The house we rented in the early '60s had three floors. My cousin and one of my buddies were down on the first floor. Me and Howard was on the second floor. And one of the neighborhood guys that wasn't any kin to us — him and his buddy was on the third floor. We were teenagers in this three-story house, just partying, enjoying life.

On the first floor — we didn't plan this — my cousin and his buddy were the drinkers, beer, wine, whiskey. So if you're a drinker, you could hang out on the first floor. On our floor, we was smoking marijuana, so if you wanted to hang out with that crowd, you come up there. And if you went up to the third floor, our buddy was selling and shooting heroin. There would be a steady stream of traffic up the steps to the heroin floor.

This is like '63. The house was always open, and it's six young guys in there, we all tight. We know everybody in the neighborhood, so nobody would come in and steal anything cause, "This is our hangout spot — don't nobody mess with it." But as we got older, it got chaotic. By the time I was eighteen, the house was just wild. Downstairs, they might be in the kitchen playing cards; upstairs, they're nodding off.

But I always kept a job. I was a short-order cook. I wouldn't say it was a good job, but I always worked.

Civil rights was deep in the middle of what was going on back then. But me and my buddies, we couldn't care less. The March on Washington took place in '63, and we were like, "Yeah, whatever." At the same time, most of the young guys in the city, and probably the young women too, had the attitude, "They're not going to smack me and I'll turn the other cheek. They can't sic dogs on me and get away with it." We weren't part of that Southern Christian Leadership generation saying, "Please, we forgive you."

No. If you hit us, we gonna throw a rock at you. That was the attitude we had. That's

46

why the cities ended up exploding. But we had no real politics.

CHAPTER 3:
WILLIAM PAUL COATES: "MY DEEPEST FEELING IS FAMILY"

A few months after Eddie Conway was born in Baltimore, Paul Coates joined the world on July 4, 1946, in Philadelphia.

Although Philadelphia, the so-called City of Brotherly Love, was founded as a religious haven for persecuted Quakers and Mennonites, the first Black people there were brought against their will, as enslaved Africans. Paul Coates, like Eddie Conway, faced, as he grew up, the multiple dilemmas embedded in what it means to be Black in the United States. He faced all the ways a seldom-acknowledged obscenity such as slavery could reverberate through generations, into his family, intricately into his own life.

Paul spent his first few years with his mother. Then he went to live with his father, who repaired TVs and radios.

My Deepest Feeling Is Family

PAUL: My mother took me to my father when I was about four, five years old. She left me there. I don't remember that I'd seen him before that. I have memories of the car ride to get to him. I have memories of leaving my bag of marbles in the car that took me there. I have memories of the smell of the car that took me to my father.

He had a television and radio repair shop. I wasn't born in a hospital; I was born on the second floor of that shop. This was in Philly, on Market Street, where Drexel [University] is now. At some point I must have gone to live with my mother, but she brought me back to that shop.

My mother had four children with my father. I had a younger brother and an older sister. My mother kept those two, while my older brother David and me went to live with my father. I lived with him until I was about nine.

My father's name was James Dudley Cryor. But for some reason, he was known to everyone as Douglas Cryor. He and my mother were never married, so I was born under her name. But up until I joined the army, I thought my name was Cryor, because after I went to live my father, he insisted on registering me in school as a

49

Cryor. When I went to the military, I had to get my birth certificate. That's when I found out my birth name wasn't Cryor. It was Coates.

The principal thing I remember about that time is my father being a television repairperson. He fixed people's TVs and radios. I think of him as similar to a computer repairperson today. When I was very young, electricity was really mysterious to me, the ohms, the amps, all of that. My father knew that stuff.

Where does somebody Black at that time learn to fix televisions and radios? He learned in some way, I still don't know how. He sat down in that early age and was able to figure it out. That would have been hard for most Black men to do at that time. I remember he used to have these screens and instruments he'd plug up to the electrical devices, testing frequencies, resistors, capacitors, tube elements and stuff, doing those strange and magical things that electrical engineers do. I remember how fascinating that was for me as a child.

My father was about educating us to the threats, how to deal with them. The police were not the largest threat; ignorance was the biggest threat. He was always pushing us to read, pushing us to think, always arguing. One of my sons, Ta-Nehisi, is a writer and he talks about how, when he came out of his house, he knew how to argue. That's straight from my father. He always kept up with the news. When I was four or five years old, he would be all about things that were in the newspaper.

"What do you think about this? You got to be able to read the paper. What do you think?" Then he would philosophize and go on forever about what he thought. He had to have his newspaper, and at that point television news was just coming into its own. I remember him lying in bed, watching the news, interrogating me about things happening in the world and challenging me with his own notions of right or wrong. Yeah, I can remember that. For him, that was at the core of getting kids across. It was all about their minds becoming alert to the world around them.

I still idolize my father in many ways. In other ways, not so much. I have come to think of him as a child molester. And someone who did not take material care of the children he created in the world. That part I don't idolize.

In addition to other children, my father had children by my mother and her two sisters. So my aunts ended up being my aunts doubly. There was Aunt Dot, then my mother. The youngest sister was Aunt Pearl. I'm convinced my father ran through the family women — but they were girls when he dealt with them.

My father would have been about twenty years older; he was probably in his thirties when he had sex with my mother. He would have dealt with my Aunt Dot maybe two years before my mother. Dot would have given birth to my brother Dudley two years before my mother — who would have been around fifteen and a half — gave birth to my older brother, David. My sister Joyce would have been born probably about the time my mother was seventeen. I would have been born when she was about nineteen. Then my youngest brother, Richard, would have been born about the time she was twenty-one. But in between David and Joyce, my father had a relationship with Aunt Pearl. So I also had a sister, Judy, who is Aunt Pearl's child. Then I'm born, and then Richard. Is that too confusing?

I don't know how those sisters managed. I just don't know how they did it. There wasn't real noticeable animosity between them about my father — if anything, there may have been some sympathy.

He was an alcoholic. I have to grapple with this — he dealt out harsh corporal punishment.

I remember there was this one time we'd gone out, we'd had a good day. My father was so happy. We came home and he was saying, "Didn't we have a good day? We did this! We did that! Didn't we have a good day?" And I was saying, "Yeah!"

Then he stopped and said, "What else?" For whatever reason, I went blank, you know. He asked, "What else? What else? What else?" I was blank.

What I remember is being picked up in the middle of my pants and being punched across the room. That actual sense of flying across the room.

I remember him beating me, I mean physically beating me as a little child. He used a belt too. I remember being so scared and running away from him. It was clear to me that I was never going to do that. Even though I did beat my kids at times; in my mind, never like him. But I don't think it mattered much. They still think I got into their butts pretty bad. We laugh about it now. Wonder would I be laughing about it with him if he was still around.

My father used to like these canned chitlins. Once, for whatever reason, he had left a can of open chitlins on the staircase. We were in the kitchen and he just went off on me. I don't know why, I can't remember now. I ran out of the kitchen and as I ran, I hit a broom that was near the can, and that can of chitlins fell. I ran up the steps and I *knew* he was going to kill me. I just knew that he was going to kill my ass.

He never came up the steps to beat me. He never came up. When I think back on this, I don't get that sensation of being hit. I get the sensation of *Black Pearl*. Aunt Pearl, my mother's sister, is the Black woman who raised me.

My memory is Pearl as my defender. I couldn't remember my mother when I finally met her again because, earlier than my mother, I remember Aunt Pearl, who used to take ass whippings for me. She would step in repeatedly and say, "Douglas, don't hit him; don't beat that child like that. Don't do that, Douglas." Then my father would go whipping on her ass. That's probably what happened with him on those steps. She would take those ass whippings over and over and over again.

You know, the deepest feeling I have from my childhood is probably family. Family.

Then We Lived in the Truck

PAUL: I must have had some early reading ability before the first grade, because I remember reading and memorizing some stuff in the Bible. I must have been good enough for my father to take me around and have me read Bible stuff in other people's houses and to his friends on the corner. He would show me off.

When I was closer to nine, my father stopped doing television repair work. I don't know if he was burned out. I know he drank a lot heavier. He used our house as a stash house.

In Philadelphia, they had a tight-controlled liquor situation. A lot of Black people — probably white people, too — operated the equivalent of speakeasies. You would go to someone's house after hours and on Sundays and buy what you wanted. So my father ran a stash house for someone who sold cheap wine, like Italian Swiss Colony. There were boxes of wine in our house, and my father would regularly drink from them. I don't remember anything being wrong with him physically, although there may have been. But one way or another, ends were not coming together. We got evicted.

Actually, we used to get eviction notices

all the time. In Philadelphia, you got a notice saying: "Sheriff's Sale." Meaning they were going to sell your stuff on the spot.

There would be a knock on the door. Then there would be some movement on the front porch, and everything would go silent. They used this paste, and they would paste this notice outside your door, saying they were getting ready to set out your stuff to be sold. We would never go outside immediately. We would wait a few minutes. If you didn't wait too long, you could strip that notice off the wall. But if you were too late, you'd be out there forever, trying to get that stuff off, and everybody would know your business. It was a dance around the constable's notice.

I remember one day when I was in elementary school. We used to come home for lunch, and on that particular day, I was with this kid who used to walk me home and then go to his house. I happened to look down my street and I saw our stuff being set out. So I told him I was going to walk him home first, and we went over to the next street.

Then I came around the corner and up on my house. My father and Aunt Pearl were loading things into the truck. I remember helping them. The hardest thing was that I had a train set that my father had bought for me. I never saw it again after we got set out. I always liked that train, you know. It was a good train set, old fashioned, heavy metal.

You talk about hard. That was hard and embarrassing. Part of a series of embarrassments. That would have been my last day in school with my father. I didn't go back.

Then we lived in the truck. My father was up against all his demons, I guess. But we stayed together in this little pickup truck he had tricked out for the purpose of collecting junk. We lived in a compartment behind these newspapers he had built up. Aunt Pearl and Judy stayed up front, then in the back of the truck, it was me, my brother Dudley, and my brother David. Altogether, there would have been six of us in that truck. May have been two weeks, maybe a little bit more. I don't think it was a month.

The last thing my father wanted to do was to drop us off at my mother's apartment. But he knew we couldn't live like that. The world had turned inward on him, so taking us back to my mother had to be one of his greatest defeats. I doubt he ever came out of that. He told me he was coming back to get me, but I think that was probably his way of coping. He never came back. Although one of my older brothers told me my father used to watch us all from a distance.

My father had impregnated those sisters, and I know he had children by other women. His manhood wasn't the equivalent of money, but his ability to be with different women perhaps gave him some type of prestige, some "you-can't-touch-this." The fact that he operated his own business, a radio and television business, probably gave him some gravity. But then to be put out, not to be able to provide for your children, and losing literally everything — that probably broke him where he wasn't broke already. Thinking back on how he was bombed out by the alcohol, I don't see how he could have got past all that. He was done.

As a child, I just wanted him to come back for me. But I can understand now, he probably never again rose any higher. When he died, he'd been living in a small rented room in South Philadelphia. He was a homicide victim. He got into an altercation with one of the guys in the gangs down there. He apparently asked this guy for a cigarette. There was some conversation and the guy beat him. My father had been in bad health, anyway. Wasn't no way he could take a beating.

I saw him at his funeral. I don't know why I didn't see him again until after he died. Part of it was probably my desire for him to be this wonderful dad, and he wasn't, at least in my mind.

He never provided for his children outside of when we lived with him. He never said, "I'm going to make sure this child gets money and shoes." But as an adult, understanding the way the world works, I have to assume that he still loved his children and he loved me. I also have to assume that he was just too damn broken to see us. He was locked with his own demons.

When I say I idolize someone, I can say, yeah, I idolized the cat. And there is this deep, deep space for him that has never been filled.

You ask why I would idolize my father? Because my father taught me the most important lesson I have. My father had all that stuff going on, but never once, to my knowledge, did he deny that any of us were his children. Not denying his children is one of the strongest memories I have.

He used to go to this house and he would pick up that child; then he would go to that house and he would pick up this child. We would all be together as brothers and sisters. My father never, never would tolerate the idea that I had a half-brother.

"This is your brother. This is your sister."

Now, he didn't take care of us after he left, and how we got here in the world may not have been the most moral way that you and I would agree with, but once we were here, he was always our father. I know that family was important to him. It became important to me, especially in having children by different mothers. Because there were times that I did not have money for my kids.

Keeping my children together and having them understand that they were brother and sister became a driving force in my life. That's the fruit I got now. That's what I got right now. My father gave that to me.

Edna Mae Coates

PAUL: I always worked. We used to work the junk truck when I was little. And I had a newspaper route. Us kids did a little bit of everything. We used to shine shoes, and me and a group of guys would head to different parts of the city and make our money at things like selling *Jet* magazine. I used to carry orders from the market for customers who bought food.

60

I worked on huckster trucks that would sell vegetables and different things, and I used to do migrant farm labor. There was a depot in North Philly, where you would go early in the morning and they would take you out to the farms in New Jersey, and you would work in the fields. I did that when I was very young for a number of years. I came up at a time when work was necessary. And my mother, she was on welfare. So I always worked. When I was growing up, I absolutely knew I wanted to be something in the world — and that meant rich. I used to walk downtown Philadelphia and touch buildings and say, "One day I'm gonna own this. Oh, fuck, yeah. One day I'm gonna travel the world."

Totally ignorant of how the world was organized against me ever, ever doing that. I guess I thought, like other folks, that being rich would give me access to travel and experiences. I saw all those narratives about other people doing it. I didn't understand that they were white narratives. I thought they included me.

My mother's name was Edna Mae Coates. She was a domestic worker. We pretty much grew up on welfare. There was no minimum wage back then; people were making fifty, seventy-five cents an hour. So she was making five dollars a day when she worked — when she could duck out from welfare. She didn't have any money and she lived in a one-bedroom apartment. She couldn't take care of four kids. We were just too much for her. That's how I ended up with my father.

As it turned out, we all went back to live with her when I was nine and my father dropped us off. She was still in a one-bedroom apartment. So she did take care of us.

I have a memory of my mother when I was older and we'd talk. She used to swear that each time she got pregnant by my father, he'd raped her. That was her story. I used to say, "Mama, Mama, come on. Be serious. Daddy raped you four times and you got pregnant each time?" She used to swear that's what happened, that he raped her. I'll never know. But that's what she insisted.

My mother's formal education was stopped when she got pregnant with my older brother David. I remember — this is me as a grown man, looking at other Black women who were educated, and admiring them so much — contrasting those women against my mother with little education. One of the women I looked up to, one of my mentors, was my mother's age. I used to look at her and think, "Wow, she could have been my mother," you know. "She could have been my mother."

But when my father brought me back to my mother, he dropped off four more people to live in that one-bedroom apartment, in addition to the kids she already had. It never occurred to me until recently that my mother easily could have said, "I can't deal with this. They've got to go someplace else."

The magnitude of her mothering is so large, compared to the smallness of my thinking, and not giving her credit, it blows me away. It's an opportunity for me to be grateful, and to be touched with gratitude for my mother and her sacrifice.

My mother passed in '91. I loved my mother and still love her, but only lately have I begun to miss and treasure her.

I Was Just so Smart
PAUL: I would have been maybe twelve, thirteen, and Martin Luther King was all in the news. There were flyers that appeared in Philadelphia, saying he was going to be at a recreational center. I remember him speaking outside to a mass of people, young and old, all from the community. Now, if you

ask me what he said, I'd have no idea. I wasn't that impressed by him, but I knew it was a historical moment. I was watching someone whose struggle was related to Black people.

I saw Malcolm a couple of times in Philadelphia, but to me at that time he was just some man that the Muslims around him in the Nation of Islam made special. Their temple was at Broad and Susquehanna. I used to carry groceries from the A&P market that was next door, and the entrance to the temple led up to the second floor. So if we got tired or bored carrying orders and we weren't making money, we would go up to their evening classes. It was ironic then and is now that on the first floor of that building was a state-controlled liquor store. And they would be upstairs preaching against the evils of liquor in the Black community while liquor was being sold downstairs.

I remember Malcolm lecturing at one of those classes. We thought it was kind of funny — women sat on one side, men on the other. They searched you before you went in, even us as little boys. We thought that was so funny, man. We sat at the back, laughing and cutting up like little kids will do.

■ ■ ■ ■

I read everything, but I used to hook school. Some of us kids would go to the main library in Philadelphia. Nobody could find you there, among all the books. There was a smaller library and an old-ass museum at 16th and Montgomery. They had some of the most wonderful artifacts. You could be in there forever. We would also go in the Philadelphia Museum of Art and Fels Planetarium. These were the places to hook in because there would always be other kids with their classes there and we did not stand out. I read all kinds of stuff like *Popular Science.* Loved comic books — read them up one side and down the other. As I got older, I loved *The Arabian Nights.* I still have a book that, unfortunately, I never returned.

I left school when I was in the tenth grade. I should have been in the twelfth grade by then, but I didn't need school, because I was just so *smart.* I thought I was smarter than everybody and everything. I knew I could get a GED and then college credits just by taking tests in the army. I don't know why I was in school anyway — I was ready for *life.* Let me go join the military!

So that's what happened.

Even before '64, when I went into the military, I started to realize that I wasn't a part of the American Dream. Philadelphia was one of the sites of race riots and before that, there were incidents between Blacks and police. Also, at that time, the Philadelphia I grew up in was controlled by street gangs, and part of going into the army was my wanting to get away from the murders. Besides, I wanted to be a John Wayne, I wanted to be an Army Ranger. All I could imagine was jumping out of airplanes, man. With my Special Forces beret. [*Laughs*] I'm glad I got over that.

Another thing, there was something about brothers who went into the service. When they came back in the community they had a walk that was different. In Philadelphia, you had to bop. You can still tell people from Philadelphia because they *bop*, you know? But these military brothers didn't have that bop — they didn't need that to walk in the community. I understand now, it was the discipline these brothers had been introduced to and it carried over to civilian life. They distinguished themselves in a different way, and I wanted a part of that. I wasn't worried about leaving my family behind. I don't think I was concerned about anyone else, I was too self-centered. *I* was the one that was getting away. Cool.

What did I do in the army? You're going to like this. I was a military policeman.

See, the army does an assessment of what you're good at, or good for. I was in basic training, in Fort Knox, Kentucky. They give you three areas that you could specialize in, so you could have a future. It actually had more to do with what the military needed. My three areas were: a military policeman who worked at White Sands Missile Base in New Mexico; a military policeman who actually was a military policeman; and finally, a military policeman who worked with sentry dogs. Those were my choices.

This came after a test. You come in, take the test, then you come back and they tell you, "Here are your options: boom, boom, and boom. What do you want?" You got maybe two minutes to say something.

I say, "Oh-god-oh-god — is that *all* I can do?" They say, "Yes." [*Laughs*]

You think they saw potential in me? They didn't see shit. They could have said, "You're a mechanic. You can work on two-and-a-half-ton diesels; you can work on tanks; you can work on shit cans. Just pick something, because you got mechanical aptitude." This is what they did to people. So I picked working with sentry dogs.

Chapter 4:
Eddie Conway: How the
Army Happened

Some people, given time, place, and circumstance, can play a quiet but decisive role in other people's lives. Howard Reed, Eddie's friend who helped start up their collective house, was also the friend who helped get Eddie into the US Army. With Howard standing as final proof that their house was becoming unglued, Eddie realized he needed a more stable life, especially now that his first child was on the way. So Eddie, like Paul, enlisted simply because the army made sense. Neither he nor Paul, nor most of the American public at the time, knew that the US military was ramping up its presence in Vietnam.

How the Army Happened
EDDIE: My friend Howard Reed was maybe a year older, but he lived in that house with me. We were childhood buddies. We would hang out and be slick guys together, the big hats, the long leather coats, the pointy shoes.

One day, Howard and I went to a movie. My girlfriend at the time, Kay Rogers — actually, my wife — was getting ready to have my first child. My father-in-law was a security guard at the movie house we went to. And Howard, he got all drunk and high at the movie, and he's making noise, so he and my father-in-law got in a beef. Because it's my father-in-law, I was able to get between them and settle the whole thing down.

So we come home — our front door is laying in the hallway. We got leather coats and big fur hats in there and all the crazy stuff that teenagers was wearing then. We even had a little .22 pistol. We come home and the door was kicked open, nobody's there. The house is empty but nothing's missing.

We ask the neighbors what's going on and they say the police raided the house. One of the girls upstairs told the cops some men there were trying to rape her. She was on drugs and had run down to the second floor and straight through our back hallway, and then she dove out the window, two stories up. There was a concrete yard, and she got all broke up. So the police had rounded up everybody in the house.

Howard and I got the door propped up

but it ain't fit. I decided that night that I'm not staying here. But Howard, he's saying, "NO. We're not leaving our stuff."

He stayed. And the police came back in the middle of the night and locked him up. The cops took him to the girl at the station house. She's all morphined up and they ask her, "Was it him?" She said, "Yes, him."

The only reason Howard didn't do forty or fifty years in jail was because he had been beefing with my father-in-law. If he hadn't had that alibi, he'd be in jail right now.

After that incident, I step back and say to myself, "Look. Kay is getting ready to have a baby. I don't want to bring a child into this world where I'm running wild."

Kay's brother was a good friend of mine. His name was Boot. Boot Rogers. So I got Boot to join the military with me. Two of my other buddies, Emanuel and Bernard, went in with us. That's pretty much how the army happened. One, Kay was pregnant; and two, there was no future for her or me or the child if I didn't get out of that environment. So three days after Kay gave birth to my son Ronald, I enlisted. September 1964, I went down with Boot Rogers and our two buddies to Fort Holabird here in Baltimore and signed up.

We were teenagers, we had no politics. No

real concern about the segregation struggles, because we thought we were in the North. That's the problem right now with Baltimore. Baltimore don't realize it's the northernmost Southern city; not the southernmost Northern city. Because we couldn't figure out where that Mason-Dixon thing runs, we never gave any thought to politics. If we had, I probably wouldn't have went into the military.

Back then, the Gulf of Tonkin had just happened. If you had said "Vietnam" to a hundred people in our neighborhood, they would have said, "What?" Wouldn't have had a clue as to where it was. In fact, almost nobody in America knew our country had gone into Vietnam. But the recruiters were like, "Hey! Come on! Here's a signing bonus!" We had no idea why it was so easy to get into the army, but *they* knew. And off to basic training they sent us.

First, I went to Augusta, Georgia for a three-month ordeal. They give you an aptitude test, to find out where you'll fit. They thought I would fit as a medic, and that was OK with me. Then each of us was sent to a different area for advance infantry training, depending on what your aptitude was. Mine was medical corpsman, so I got sent to Fort Sam Houston, in San Antonio,

Texas. I really wanted to learn this stuff. My main concern was: "I don't want to be the only person that's stupid."

I had no idea that all the rest of *them* was stupid.

There was maybe four months of advanced training, medical school, and then they shipped me and Emanuel to Germany. I was going over there to run a MASH [mobile army surgical hospital] unit, with the triage and helicopters and stuff.

They shipped Boot and Bernard out to Vietnam. This was maybe early 1965, and the government was just starting their military buildup. So I end up in Europe and my brother-in-law end up in Vietnam. He never came back.

Potatoes for You Motherfuckers

EDDIE: There were racist things going on against the Black population in the military — I started seeing that over in Germany. I was in a platoon of twenty-five people, twenty-two of them were white. There was one Black sergeant, then there was Goodman, a Black PFC [private first class]. Goodman was the division boxing champ — so he's already my best friend, right? [*Laughs*] Goodman was my only peer. He and I were in there with all those white soldiers. And it started off really bad.

The first morning, we're standing in formation, getting details on who's going to peel the potatoes today; who's going to dig the ditches; wash out the latrine; who's going to wax the general's ass. That kind of stuff. Maybe ten platoons are lined up. Most of the sergeants were from the South. They were old; they were racist. They tried to cover that up but it would always come out. So the officers are saying, "We want two people from each platoon."

They get two from one platoon and those people are Black. The next platoon, they get two more and those guys just happen to be Black — all the way up to our platoon, which was maybe number nine. This white sergeant, he's like [*shading eyes, makes pretend search-over-assembled-troops*], "Uh, Goodman. Conway." I'm a newbie, it's not a big deal. So off I go to KP [kitchen patrol] duty. That went on for almost two weeks. Every time, two Black guys get sent out.

Here's something that I don't tell everybody. I had started looking historically, at Columbus, at the conquistadores, at what happened to the Native Americans. I studied and I used to just beat the white guys in the head about stuff they were saying that was wrong.

I mean they swore to God that Columbus discovered America or that there were only five continents. Stupid shit, stuff that was absolutely ridiculous. But they said it with such authority. Like, "The Indians were savages when we got here. They were scalping people." I would correct them, then it would get to where we would go get a book and I would show them, and they were [*miming dumb acquiescence*], "Uh — OK."

One day I'm like: "Wait. I'm digging ditches. I'm peeling potatoes. I'm washing toilets. I'm doing all this stuff in a platoon with a bunch of idiots."

On this day, the lieutenant's standing out there, coming up the ranks, picking out the Black guys for duty. He's saying, "Uh, medical platoon. Give me two men." And I just burst out, "Let CONWAY go! Yeah, let him do it!"

Of course, everybody is shocked. You're standing at attention; you're not supposed to make any noise. They end up sending somebody else, and the lieutenant tells me, "You are going to the company commander's office."

By then I was thoroughly pissed off — I had just *had* it. If the commander had given me trouble, I would have jumped on him. So I went straight on in there and I said, "Look, I've been in this damn company for two weeks. I haven't had a chance to get a haircut or shave. I don't know where the PX [post exchange] is. I didn't join the army to peel fucking potatoes for you motherfuckers."

Assassination Based on a True Story

EDDIE: It took me about a year and a half, but by the time I was twenty I was a sergeant. I was what's called a Physicians Assistant's Equivalent. I'm a Black GI Joe working in emergency rooms, doing first aid. I'm basically running the platoon, but I was never shooting people.

Because the Black soldiers from the other units knew about me, they would come to me with their problems. This was the first time in my life I was actually counseling and caring for people. I found a happiness in that. Later, I was doing that in the Panthers and teaching Panthers how to take care of injuries. In fact, in prison, I had to stop myself because there was a kind of medical hat I would slip on if something happened to the comrades — we had about a hundred comrades in there. I would turn into a medic, you know.

But in the army, I envisioned myself help-ing to fight the Vietnamese. They were com-mies, yeah. And we were fighting for democ-racy, making the world safe. Sure, America had problems, there was some racism in the military, but America seemed to us to be the most advanced country in the world.

For example, Germany was supposed to be a very modern country, but we saw Germans still going to the bathroom in outhouses. We were so arrogant, we would say, "Next month when I get a thirty-day leave, I'm going back to the world" — meaning America. Everything outside America wasn't really the world. That's the mentality they promote in the service.

The stuff they make you do — even in Germany. We weren't in wartime, but we would actually ride tanks through people's houses. There was one time a whole column of us was going down a hill and one tank took a sharp left turn. The tank was going so fast that, when it turned, it slid into a house. I wasn't in that tank; I was in a medi-cal armored personnel carrier maybe five or six tanks behind.

You're doing fifty miles in a tank that weighs fifty-some tons — a huge monstros-ity, and the driver loses control and you go right through somebody's house. If they're in there, they're dead or injured. This time, it didn't kill anybody — it just pretty much wrecked the house.

Behind every column is an officer, a paymaster. He assesses the damage and writes a check there on the spot. Some little lieutenant with a checkbook says, "OK, the new value of your house is five grand." And because the people got paid, they're legally not able to say anything.

The shocking thing for me was realizing that Germany was occupied. You can drive through somebody's house, maybe kill their animals, kill their child. The officer on the end comes up, signs the check, and you'll never hear about it in the States. I mean, these are white people, right? And these Germans were — cowering.

After I made sergeant, I had my own jeep. That meant I could go anywhere I wanted. Also. I was selling hash. I was a crook. [*Laughs*] We was going into Sweden and buying hash and bringing it to Copenhagen and smuggling it into Germany. I had to do something with the profits, so I was loan-sharking the money out to the old sergeants who were alcoholics — by the fifteenth of the month, they'd drunk up all their pay.

In Copenhagen and places outside Germany where people were fleeing the military, there was political education and organizing. But also, in Europe, most news and the American music they were playing was a year or two behind. Even then, it was filtered in the army newspapers, so a lot of important information wasn't getting to us. The Black Panther Party wasn't on the horizon. Black militancy itself was an attitude but not any kind of formation; it was just angry Black people. So I did not hear that Malcolm X had been assassinated till '66. In fact, I didn't know who Malcolm X was.

I was in Copenhagen, taking my date to a play called *Patrick X.* At the theater, they got little books out, saying this play is based on a true story. So this Patrick X character gets assassinated and I'm like, *Huh?* Damn, a Black man assassinated? In America? Yeah, we get killed. Black men are lynched and shot to death. We get pianos dropped on us — but a political *assassination* — why?

Of course, then I learned about Malcolm X. So I started looking at Malcolm's writing. Damn, this is some serious stuff here. But even then, I thought that America was the best thing that ever happened to the world. I knew there was racism, knew there was an imbalance. But I didn't attribute it to capitalism. I didn't attribute it to American history. The America thing was still good to go in my head.

Eventually, I hooked up with a bunch of young Black Africans. Back then, Africans were welcomed in Denmark, in the Scandinavian countries. I don't even know where these brothers were from — they were just so angry with Americans, with white people. But they also were mad with us Black servicemen. They would cross the street rather than walk beside us. They said we sided with the white man. I didn't understand. I thought they were angry because they didn't have nothing. I just didn't know *why* they didn't have nothing.

I'm in the Wrong Army

EDDIE: Then I got a letter from Kay. She wrote that Boot had been killed in Vietnam. He got ambushed in a rice paddy. I was so hurt by that. I felt responsible. Had it not been for me, my brother-in-law would have never gone into the military. And I'm over here in Germany, safe. This is my fault. I'm like, OK, I got to go over and revenge his death.[1]

That's why I signed up for Vietnam, even after reading Malcolm X and seeing all this racism. I'm mad about my brother-in-law,

80

and I'm still convinced that America's OK. So I was filling out the papers and ready to go. Until I had a final turning point.

One morning, I'm setting there with my uniform all laid out, reading the army paper, *Stars and Stripes.* On the front page is a photo of Black women on a street corner in Newark, and in the center of the street there's an Army personnel carrier. This was a picture of the so-called Newark Riot. I saw one of those box tanks with the treads, right? On top of that thing is a 50-caliber machine gun and a belt of bullets, the kind we used to wear around our neck, pointed at these Black women. I woke up.

Because, one: being a medic, I knew the damage that those 50-caliber bullets could do, and two: I knew the weapon. I knew that if you pressed that button, it would go off twenty-five to fifty times before you could stop it. I looked at that weapon, and I looked at the women. This little white soldier is setting up in that tank and he's pointing at these Black women.

I look over to my uniform, all starched and pressed. The boots are shining, and I'm ready to put this stuff on and go out. I say, "No. Something is wrong here. The army is not supposed to be in the middle of a Black community with machine guns pointed at

Black women. One of them could be my mom."

I was in shock. I went outside — which is a no-no — in my bathrobe. Even though I'm now a sergeant, I know I ain't got no business out there like that. I say to the Black soldiers, "Did you all see this?"

They say, "Yeah, I seen it."

They were like, "Oh yeah, another riot in the cities."

I went and told my commanding officers, "I'm in the wrong army. I'm not going to Vietnam, I'm taking a leave."

Even though I'd been living the life of Riley, having a ball where I was, I took a thirty-day leave and just vacated the premises. In fact, I refused to put on a uniform. The only time I put on that uniform again was when I had to come back to sign out.

CHAPTER 5:
PAUL COATES: I BECAME,
TO MYSELF, BLACK

PAUL: I'm a child of the sixties, I'm born into seeing Black people beaten, being hosed on television. At the same time — more in real life than on television — I'm seeing a Muslim response to that. This tells me I'm different and there are two realities. You see, I still don't think I understood the division of Black and white. I knew there was a difference but back then I had no real sense of the hypocrisy in society. I had some awareness that I didn't have control, but I think I probably sensed it as just plain and deep vanilla.

When I got into the military, I assumed I was as qualified and capable as anyone else. But the military confirmed that was not the case. The "why" of it was the beginnings of my political consciousness. There was a moment in the army that I became, to myself, Black. I know the moment.

I was the only Black in an almost all-white

unit. And I had a conflict with this Native American, who the white boys called "Chief." One day, I came from the chow hall and went into the day room, which is like a general recreation room. We had day rooms on each floor with maybe a common television, a pool table, a few books, things like that. This day room I walked into was the largest one in the building that everybody came into.

So I walk in and this Native American guy starts off by calling me nigger. I'm confronted by him. I'm also confronted by all these white folks. So I have to go at him. We tussle, we fall over a couch. Then we get separated by this white guy — which is real interesting because we called him Tex and he has all the traits that I'd learned were Southern and racist. His language got the longest drawl and a twang, and he's calling the guy, "Chief."

"Chief, what's wrong with you?" Chief was still talking this nigger stuff, and Tex was saying, "So what? So what that he's Black?" Until that moment, I don't know that I'd been ever called "Black" by a white person.

"So what if he's Black?" Tex was saying. "You're red and I'm white. What does that got to do with it?" Somehow, he separated us and sent the Native American guy off.

I'm shaken. I go upstairs and lock my door. I realize I can't stay there. I got to come out of my room because I'm concerned now that these cats are going to jump me. I go into the day room on my floor to be ready to fight in the open and I encounter this book. The book is *Black Boy.* I don't even remember referring to myself as a Negro then. I just knew that there was *not* a book called, *Black Boy.* I thought they were playing a joke on me. I decide to take the bait. I read a few pages and it looks legit. I put the book under my arm, and I go back to my room and start reading Richard Wright's book. I'd read Black books before — Baldwin was popular — but even before I finished reading *Black Boy,* I realized that I identified with the Blackness in the narrative. It became clear to me that there were other books like this.

Right before *Black Boy,* though, I was reading the Marquis de Sade and other European "classics." I also had a passion for stories about Black veterans. I felt grounded in historical novels, books of science, things like that. I don't know that I was all that impressed by Richard Wright. I was more impressed that he made me think about other books like that, and I could and *should* have access to them. Because I hadn't known about Richard Wright and writers like Countee Cullen or Langston Hughes. I felt terribly ignorant. What *Black Boy* did was to make me aware of a genre. I decided that I would specialize, that I would read until I mastered that genre. So I began a serious pursuit of Black books. That was my conscious evolution. My identity came from books and that fight that day.

Coming alive and awake was realizing that separation point between me and "them." It's a strange thing, how you separate white folks as white folks. Because then you have to go back and re-separate. Like, I knew the contradiction of Tex, a white boy, separating me and Chief. And even though I came out of that incident Black, and could look at "white" as being this monolith, I also saw difference within that monolith.

It's like Malcolm explaining white after he comes back from Mecca. Malcolm says, "Over there, I met white people who had blue eyes, but that didn't mean they thought they was boss." That's not verbatim, of course.

I remember where I was when Malcolm X was assassinated. I was in a car with a bunch of other Black army guys, headed for town. About four, five o'clock in the afternoon, Texas time, it came on the radio: "Malcolm X, the fiery Black Muslim leader, has been killed in New York."

I remember the guys kept talking, and I said, "Wait a minute, did you hear that? Malcolm X got killed." There may have been one other person in that car who had some vague inkling — who knew who Malcolm X was.

Hooked Up with the Panthers

PAUL: I enlisted for thirty-six months, and spent about nineteen months in Vietnam. I probably served in about six different places, mid-country, high-country, to the South.

The thing to get is that for most GIs, Vietnam was not fighting in the rice paddies. You can't have everybody fighting all the time, because you have to support the troops. You need doctors, nurses, supply companies, engineers to build the roads. The war was going on outside the cities, but most of us GIs spent time in or near urban areas, because that's where the bases were. I was in one or two military bases that got attacked, but as a sentry dog trainer, I was on the far reaches of the base. So Vietnam was not bad to me.

I had no intention of staying in the military; all I wanted to do was find my place in America. When I got out, I was probably twenty years old. I'm smart and I'm going to have a business and I'm going to do this and that. But then something changed.

I got back to the States, and I didn't want to be here. I wanted to be back in Vietnam. I was trying to figure out how to get back . . . [*long pause*]

If I had made it back, I probably could have lived there. I had met a woman I cared for. I had met a people I was comfortable with. At the same time, I had already met Linda, the woman in the States who was going to be my wife. So I was betwixt and between. I would have gone back to Vietnam as a contractor. I had no consciousness then of the role contractors played in Vietnam. I would have gone there in defense of imperialistic efforts. But it worked out that my attraction for Linda led me to come to Baltimore. Kelley was my first-born child, a girl. Linda was pregnant with Kris, my second daughter, when I got hooked up with the Panthers in the early fall of '69.

CHAPTER 6:
CRAZY AS THE
WORLD IS CRAZY

When Eddie and Paul came back from the Army, each had to start whole new lives: find jobs, places to live, set up families, reconnect with friends. And then, of course, there were the Panthers. Eddie joined the Baltimore Panther Party, even though his old pal Howard Reed couldn't feature it. Paul came later to the Panther scene in Baltimore. The Black Panther Party, standing defiantly for justice, even liberation, helped shape and focus Eddie's and Paul's lives — along with the lives of thousands of other young African Americans.

Speaking of "young": people nowadays, looking back over the decades at the Panthers' militant politics and the life-and-death situations they often faced, usually don't realize how very young most of the Panthers were. When Paul and Eddie came to the Party, they were still in their early twenties.

Don't Say Nothing Around Conway

EDDIE: When I went home, I moved from Black GI Joe to hopeful, reformist Negro. I joined the NAACP. Based on the civil rights movement, I said, "OK, there's problems and the best way to deal with them is to continue to integrate."

That's how I became a fire fighter. Because they hadn't been letting Blacks in the fire department — or the police department or into engineer management. All those solid jobs with good pay, they weren't letting Blacks into, so we were integrating them at the end of '67 and early '68.

Down at Sparrows Point, where the steel mill is — they're dismantling it now — I and five other Blacks, we integrated the fire department. There were 105 firemen — which means there was ninety-nine white guys. So there I was, integrating.

I would walk into the firehouse at the end of the shift and there'd be twenty-five white guys in there, talking about jungle bunnies and killing them. I'd catch them selling guns to each other, and I started looking at those guys. These were good ol' white boys, organizing networks. They were armed, and before they realized what I was about, they would talk around me. "Yeah, them welfare queens" — this is their socialization. I would push back and straighten them out. I'd say, "There's more white welfare queens than Black, you know."

Later, when I walk into the department, all conversations stop. By then, I'm an angry Black man. I'm not associated with any group, but I got a bush haircut and I am not for a whole lot of shit. I got a big mouth and anything I hear wrong I challenge. The word is out: "Don't say nothing around Conway."

They finally stopped talking around me, but I would still catch them. They were armed to the teeth, they were all around the city, and they were saying, "If there's a riot, or if they come around here, we're going to kill them. And if they fight back, we'll just get rid of all of them."

I'm like, WHOA. Get rid of all of *who*? It was that right-wing, white conservative attitude, that kind of fascism, that drove me straight to the Left. "No, we'll fight back."

After the death of Martin Luther King, I moved from "We can reform this" to "This can't be reformed." There was a problem that wasn't only in this or that city; it was clear across the whole country.

I Became a Community Worker

PAUL: The army was the beginning of my consciousness. I didn't take the military to heart; I took commitment to heart. One of the main things I got back then — and it was reinforced when I got into the Black Panther Party — was a sense of mission. To see your mission as a commitment to what you set out to do, to something higher than yourself. The military drives that into you, and the Panther Party drove that home, too. When you say you're going to show up, you do it — I took all that to heart. I took to heart that people depended on you.

I got attracted to the Panthers because, as my consciousness developed, the impulse to do something in the world increased — as I read more Black books, as I began to notice and become more aware, the desire to contribute grew in me.

I looked for organizations to join. I'd read about the Panthers, but that was a distant thing in California. I didn't know about a lot of organizations in Baltimore, so I went to join the organizations in Washington. I went to the Republic of New Afrika in DC, but they were closed. I went to the SNCC [Student Nonviolent Coordinating Committee] office, but they also had closed. There were other Black organizations with

92

headquarters in DC, but all of them had closed, so I came back to Baltimore still feeling this need. Then one night me and a partner were hanging out, and we ran into this sister who claimed to be a Panther. She agreed to take me past the Panther office so I would know where it was.

After a couple of weeks, I went back, knocked on the door. They looked at me like I was crazy. They looked me all up and down because they thought I was a pig, an agent that had been sent there, so they didn't let me in.

I came back later and they did let me in. I got to know a couple of them at that early point. That would have been in the early fall of '69.

So I became a community worker. In fact, "community worker" was a designation, because at that point, the Panthers had closed the rolls and weren't admitting more people. Many people *thought* they were Panthers, when they were really community workers. But community workers sold newspapers; we did most of the things that Panthers did.

Doing What Needs to Be Done

EDDIE: There was talk of Black Power, self-determination, even Black capitalism. Me and a couple of my buddies had already started checking out different Black organizations. The nationalist thing didn't work with me because half of my friends were white. The model-cities thing wasn't militant enough. There were some Black Nationalist army formations that seemed too rigid. Eventually, the Panthers looked like it was a group that was doing what needed to be done.

I wasn't really aware of the Panther Party when I was in the army. I came in contact with the Panthers by reading the *Black Panther* newspaper. Once I started reading it, I began to think, "We need something to protect our community, something that will take us to a different level of struggle, so we can change our conditions."

Howard Reed, my buddy — the guy I lived with in that house — we were hanging out again after I got home from the service. Howard talked more Black-talk than anybody you ever seen. But he wouldn't pick up a shovel and plant one flower for the Black community. He was always like that. So when he and I went to look at the Black Panther Party, I said, "I'm going to get in here and see if I can help." But he said, "Naw, I'm not messin' with them."

Howard wouldn't break a grape, but I was

going to join it.

That's How They Rose

PAUL: Back in the day, I really believed there was going to be a revolution next week. The Black Panthers gave me that belief. I'm not saying that to blame the Panthers. The situation as I saw it — the objective conditions at that time — was that something needed to be done. I saw The Revolution as being imminent. It would just take a little more work to tip society in that direction. I accept full responsibility for misdiagnosing that situation. [*Laughs big*]

Here's what Ta-Nehisi writes about the Black Panthers in his book, *The Beautiful Struggle:*

It took all kinds, bourgeois college students, teenage mothers, plumbers, and professors. But the beloved and honored foot soldiers hailed from the back end of the world. They were the risen armies of the dead — cutthroats, rapists, brigands, and murderers — who in other lives feasted on their own people's toil. [79]

I think he captures it pretty good. But the beloved foot soldiers weren't only the "risen armies of the dead." Some of the leadership

95

were from those armies of the dead, too.

Yes, there were some saints but there were also some cold-up criminals. But could any revolutionary group be other than that? I mean really, quote-unquote "revolutionary"? It takes your criminals; it takes your college students, and it takes those people who feasted on their own people. That's how they rose; that's where they come from.

Do I think the Panthers changed the criminals so they stopped feasting on their own people? Sometimes they did. Many times they did not. That's how you would explain the infiltrators in the Panther Party. They were feasting on their own people. That's how you would explain people in the Panther Party sometimes being murderous thugs.

That's how you would explain Huey P. Newton. He was not above that, but he put things into a political context. I got that. But I don't know if he's so different from other criminals who have made movements work throughout the world.

I'm defending the Panthers from people who say they were total criminals. That's just not accurate. But it wouldn't be accurate if you said they were saints, either. The Panthers weren't some God-spoken group that came out of the mist. That's who the Panthers were. Those were the people that I knew, the people I grew up with. They were just as crazy as the world is crazy. If you took a sampling of any slice of society today — like we walk down the street and gather ten people — that's who would be in the Panther Party. You'd have prostitutes who maybe stopped prostituting because of the politics. You'd have robbers and thieves, and you'd have college and high school students, workers, and activists because, more likely than not, those are the people that first raised their hands about changing society. They're on the bottom, they got the least, so they got the most to gain by changing the situation. The folks on the top have least to gain. But they're still robbers and crooks, too.

I was an idealist. But I still couldn't envision the ideal revolutionary society we said we wanted to create. Hell no, never. No one I knew in the Panther Party envisioned an ideal, either.

White folks probably had a more concrete thing because their vision ended largely with, STOP THE WAR IN VIETNAM! But it wasn't like they had this ideal of how society was going to transform. Like the anti-apartheid movement: END APARTHEID NOW! There's nothing that comes after that.

But at least those are concrete goals.

In the case of the Panther Party, we never had that end goal. We always fell back on the will of the people: "All that shit going to get worked out after the Plebiscite."

I don't know that this is a failing of the Left, except maybe in the sense that the Left feels it needs to put forth a vision that's radically different than what already is. But even if a movement is right-wing, their vision is not necessarily going to be what results, other than some repression — which actually comes from the Left also. Let's face it, the Right does not have a lock on repression.

It's hard for people to come up with the notion of what society needs to be, isn't it? It's a hard job. And from my perspective, we did not have it.

Panthers Having a *Real* Party

EDDIE: I started looking at the Panther programs and how the Panthers were organizing. The *Black Panther* newspaper was probably the most serious recruiting tool. Then when I looked at the actual Panther Party office in Maryland, it was night and day. Oh yeah. They were not the Party the paper said they should have been.

When I got there, the Panthers were having a *real* party. The girls running up the steps and swinging across the room on chandeliers and hollering, "Weeee!" And the guys running up behind them, "Weeee!" Like, what the fuck?

Initially, I never suspected anybody infiltrating. So I go to California, then to New York to train. I think maybe Afeni Shakur, Tupac's mother, might have trained us. There were military aspects that I'd learned in the army, a pecking order, drills. I have to say that all of that served me well because I trained Panthers in first aid, weapons, all of that stuff I learned from the military.

Most of the Panthers were young teenagers, but there was a lot of veterans in the Panthers. In fact, those in their twenties were probably veterans. So I get trained, and eventually, being gung ho, I end up becoming Lieutenant of Security.

You got to have discipline to have an organization. If you want to serve breakfast in the morning to a hundred children, you can't be partying all night long. But there was something really wrong with this Baltimore picture.

What was wrong with that picture, it turned out, was that the government had set the chapter up. But I assumed at the time, because everybody was so young, that people just didn't have any discipline. There were serious people here and there; enough for the Party to be a serious entity. But the members weren't reading and studying. I said, "OK, this needs to be fixed."

■ ■ ■ ■

PART II

■ ■ ■ ■

Our resistance gave us an identity. Our identity gave us strength. Our strength gave us an unbreakable will.
— Albert Woodfox, *Solitary: My Story of Transformation and Hope*

CHAPTER 7:
THEY USED OUR PEOPLE TO KILL OUR PEOPLE

Nobody knows how most radical liberation movements of the past might have played out — the innovative good they might have done; the interesting mistakes they might have made — because the US government and its many surveillance agencies were hell-bent on shutting them down at every turn. If you'd come to Earth from a more enlightened planet, you might think that the United States of America, touting itself as the beacon of equality and freedom, would encourage political movements wanting more justice. But justice for literally everybody is a horrifying prospect to a power structure whose wealth and strength depend on centuries of actualized inequality.

As the civil rights movement grew into Black power, surveillance agencies saw an upsurge in political organizing that posed a direct threat to the realpolitik underlying "liberty and justice for all." Law enforcement agencies intensified campaigns of monitoring, infiltration, and disinformation that were already fairly intense. The best known of these efforts was the Federal Bureau of Investigation's Counterintelligence Program, or COINTELPRO. This was the same program that likely played an outsized role in the formation of the Baltimore Panther Party, and was to misshape most of Eddie Conway's adult life.

COINTELPRO began in 1956 as part of a US campaign to crush the "Soviet menace." Later, as the civil rights movement, the feminist movement, and opposition to the war in Vietnam grew, COINTELPRO widened its anti-Communist sweep, targeting newer domestic organizations such as the American Indian Movement, the Student Nonviolent Coordinating Committee, antiwar coalitions, and any Black civil rights, nationalist, or liberation group — none of which was deemed more ominously "un-American" than the Black Panther Party for Self-Defense.

The Panthers often attracted thousands of Black people to their rallies. But these thousands stood for millions, according to a 1970 Harris poll reporting that 25 percent of African Americans felt that the Panthers reflected their own views.[1] J. Edgar Hoover, who had already issued orders to "expose, disrupt, misdirect, discredit, or otherwise neutralize" troublesome groups, now fixated on the Panthers in an FBI memo instructing fourteen field offices to "submit imaginative and hard-hitting counterintelligence measures aimed at crippling the BPP."[2] The FBI's measures also metastasized into a lethal collaboration with other federal agencies, such as the Department of Defense and the National Security Agency (NSA), and with local police departments.

One of the government's gentler methods of neutralizing the Panthers was a misinformation campaign. Agents sent forged letters, offensive cartoons, and death threats to Party members. Panthers would receive phony communiqués, ostensibly from trusted leaders, accusing them of betrayal. Bulletins and flyers appeared, announcing public events, but with the wrong time and place, leading communities that needed services like the Free Breakfast Program to think that the Panthers were shifty and undependable.

Following up on this was an FBI classic, *The Black Panther Coloring Book*. Here, children were asked to color in the drawings of rugged African American freedom fighters shown stabbing, punching, and shooting white cops and businessmen, usually drawn as having pig-heads. The coloring book was sent to companies that had donated food to the Free Breakfast Program. Years passed before anyone learned that it had been designed and distributed by the FBI.[3]

Neutralization could also be upfront and violent. Without warning or reason, Panther offices across the country were blown up, friends and family threatened, disappeared, tortured, murdered. Meanwhile, the public got a sinister, sensationalized view of the Panthers through mainstream media, which regaled the world with breathless accounts of Panther-vs.-police shootouts.[4]

In Chicago, Fred Hampton, beloved and formidably charismatic Panther leader, was shot to death at age twenty-one, along with BPP member Mark Clark, during a police raid on Hampton's apartment in the early hours of December 4, 1969. Although the police claimed and the press initially described the incident as a shootout, it was later proven that the Panthers had fired only once — seemingly accidentally — while the police fired at least eighty-two shots into Hampton's home. Investigations showed that these murders were a joint effort involving the Chicago police and federal intelligence, and that Hampton had been drugged by a government informant who had infiltrated the BPP.[5]

There were also over-the-top prosecutions of fabricated terror plots. Such a case was that of the Panther 21, in which most of the

New York Panther Party leadership spent two years in jail on bogus charges of conspiring to blow up department stores, the Bronx Botanical Gardens, and other key sites in New York City.

The fact that the jury in the Panther 21 trial took only forty-five minutes to acquit every defendant in the case must have been a blow to COINTELPRO's dream of a world free of Black militancy. After the Panther 21, prosecutions didn't stop, but they were usually more carefully crafted, less likely to fail.

What the feds seemed to want, if they couldn't arrange actual deaths, was a virtual Panther-to-prison pipeline. Nationally, the reality for the Panthers, their friends and families, became a roiling onslaught of wrongful arrests set up by agents posing as diehard radicals.

Part of why COINTELPRO was so effective was that, although Panther members certainly knew things were going wrong, no one quite knew where the damage was coming from, or how extensively people were being targeted. Young people who had grown up, usually poor and disrespected, who felt they'd found a new way to create a more just world, were seeing the hope of that world fall apart.

Years later, Eddie Conway remembers:

It all seemed random. I didn't know I had an FBI Counterintelligence Program file. Of course, nobody knew about COINTEL-PRO back then. So I was thinking my case was a local phenomenon.

Eddie sees what the Panthers went through in a global context:

The Panthers weren't the only ones. You also had Students for a Democratic Society, the antiwar movement, millions of people across the world, the Vietnamese, students and labor unions shutting Paris down, the PLO [Palestine Liberation Organization] in Palestine, the Algerians winning some independence. There was enough worldwide understanding of revolution for us to see that we were getting hammered. But we couldn't fully understand the scope, because it looked like individual coyote acts.

So the Chicago police get off the hook for Fred Hampton's murder. And some crazy nationalist in Los Angeles assassinates two of our people: Bunchy Carter and John Huggins.[6] Somebody — probably the Klan — blows up our office in Des Moines, Iowa.[7] Twenty-one Panthers in New York City get locked up — we know that somebody had to set them up. But these looked like random acts.

After Eddie got locked up, he had years to study all this. *"There were Black Panther Parties in thirty-seven states,"* he says:

In eighteen months, the government basically wiped out the Panther Party in twenty-five of those states. In Texas, one of the leaders was just standing outside somewhere and a sniper shot him in the head from blocks away. In San Diego, they killed four of our people; in Oakland, there was the guy buried in the bomb factory. They used our people to kill our people. They ran people out of the country. They locked up the ones that wouldn't leave.

The Panthers were able to remain militant because they remained essentially optimistic. *"For us,"* says Eddie, *"it was, 'OK, we can get ourselves together' ":*

It honestly looked like we could — there was enough young energy to push it forward. We were thinking, "Love your people; let's network, build." Because there were white people doing the same thing; there were Latinos, Indians, Puerto Ricans, the women's movement, old people was organizing. They were saying, "We can have a better world — it's possible." We partly thought this because we could look overseas at places like Angola and they were fighting. We could look at South Africa, South America, France, Vietnam . . .

Eddie and Paul — and thousands in their generation — believed that The Revolution was on the way. One indication of that was that "The Black Panther Party for Self-Defense" did, in fact, mean fighting police beatings and shootings that were routine in most African American communities. Nowadays, the simple mention of "Black Panthers" to the general public calls up stock-photo images of militant Black predators in frightening, gun-toting poses. What is forgotten is that "Self-Defense" also meant nurturing, protecting, and caring for people in Black communities.

In Baltimore, Eddie helped start a food co-op that provided low-cost groceries to neighborhoods, as well as needed revenue for the Panthers. The Baltimore chapter also created the People's Health Clinic, which, changing hands over the years, lasted until 2015, when it finally went bankrupt.[8] And, in the basement of the St. Martin de Porres Community Center,

Eddie's chapter set up its Free Breakfast Program to feed hungry children.

Nationally, the Free Breakfast Program is probably the best-known community work of the Panther Party. But as a whole, the Party launched more than thirty-five community programs, including free healthcare clinics, ambulance and transportation services, education, and legal aid — most of which proved more threatening than mere guns to the government's concept of the American way of life. In fact, Hoover's famous description of the Panthers as "the greatest threat to internal security of this country" appeared in a 1969 FBI memo, in which he denounced the malevolent influence of the Free Breakfast Program on "impressionable youths."[9]

So Paul and Eddie met in the Baltimore chapter of the Black Panther Party. More importantly, they met during the height of COINTELPRO.

CHAPTER 8:
GIVE US THAT MAN!

EDDIE: Sometimes there were zealots causing trouble in the Panther Party, but mainly people causing trouble were working for the government. Right here in Baltimore City, a fight occurred up the corner from our office. One of the Panthers started running down the street; the police ran chasing him. He ran into our office, locked the doors, ran out the back.

The police pull up — *screeeeee* — all around our office.

"GIVE US THAT MAN!"

"We ain't got that man."

"COME OUT WITH YOUR HANDS UP!"

"*Hell,* no."

Of course, we get locked up.

We go to court. Guess who's on the stand? Yep. The guy that ran down the street, in our door, and out the back.

They had to let everybody go because the

Baltimore Sun investigated it and found out this guy was working for the Baltimore Police Department. How could the Panthers be responsible for harboring a fugitive when the fugitive was a police employee?

So you had good people trying to do good work with the community, and then you had the government undoing that work every chance they got. We were definitely receiving the pointed end of the spear . . .

Back in the day, it was my job to check people's backgrounds and make sure the Panther office was secure. That led me to start investigating this guy named Warren Hart, who was the Baltimore defense captain. That's when I started to become aware that the chapter was infiltrated, because all the things going wrong couldn't have happened without Warren Hart allowing it.

For instance, one of our Panthers went out in the middle of the day and robbed something, and got killed. There was no rhyme or reason to it. So I back-checked and I found that Hart had told him to do that. I realized at that point that this guy was working for somebody else. All roads stopped with Warren Hart. Then I found out that he wasn't who he said he was — but I couldn't find out who he was. This is maybe a year before my own case started, right Paul?

PAUL: Let me go back. I wasn't in the Party at that time, so this is based on my research. Eddie calls in a team of Panthers who came in to straighten out the Baltimore chapter. They'd gotten reports from Eddie and from other people.

EDDIE: I got a team to come down from New York with Arthur Turco, who was this white defense lawyer, and Donald Cox — we called him DC — and Captain Mitch, that's Henry Mitchell. California also sent folks to investigate, and when they got there, Warren fled.

PAUL: Right. It's possible he had been tipped off. He never showed up at the chapter.

EDDIE: At the time, we didn't know where Hart went; he just disappeared from the United States of America. Turns out he joined the All African People's Revolutionary Party in Canada. Evidently, when Warren left here, the FBI contacted the Mounties and told them he was a good infiltrator. So he worked for the Mounties up there. We found this out by running his picture

114

in the paper. Eventually our contacts in Canada found him in their midst. After we discovered him, he fled to the Caribbean and got a couple of people killed down there. We still didn't know what he was up to. We knew he was an agent provocateur, but we didn't know he worked for the National Security Agency until later.

There was a Canadian hearing [Royal Commission of Inquiry Concerning Certain Activities of the Royal Canadian Mounted Police, or "McDonald Commission"] that Warren was forced to testify for in the late '70s. He talked about all the stuff he did and that's how we finally put a label on him.

PAUL: But the part with Turco and them being here in Baltimore ties into Eugene Anderson being killed. Anderson was the man that ended up dead in the park.[1]

EDDIE: Yeah. There was a horrible case in 1969 where this Panther, Eugene Anderson, was tortured and his body was dumped in Leakin Park. We don't know that that was really his body, because the FBI first reported it as a thirty-year-old white male, then they said it was a twenty-year-old Black male. But Anderson may have been one of the police informers.

PAUL: We don't know who Eugene Anderson was. I'm not sure how much he'd hung around the Panthers. I can't remember where this comes from, but I think Anderson had had some relation to the sister of the person who fingered him as a police informant — who was himself a police informant. I don't know those details; it's questionable whether Anderson was an informant. But the people who tortured him were. Many of them left the torture sessions and went out to report to their handlers. It was crazy.

EDDIE: There was something like that happening about the same time in New Haven. Got Bobby Seale and Ericka Huggins swept up.[2] And in Chicago, when they assassinated Fred Hampton — that informant, William O'Neal, who drew the floor plans of Fred's apartment for the cops — he's the one that put an electric chair in the basement of one of our headquarters. To shock people and make them "confess."[3]

PAUL: But in Baltimore, Turco and them were in and out of the Panther house in some kind of way during the time Anderson was held there. They would eventually all be charged in that murder.

The case eventually went away, because of Larry Gibson, who was a lawyer representing Charles Wyche, one of the defendants. Gibson exposed that there were at least six other agents in the Baltimore chapter who participated in the beating and torture of the police informant — who may never have been an informant. Like Eddie said, Hart was sent to Canada.

EDDIE: The cops charged almost everybody with murder or accessory before or after the fact. They locked up the whole leadership. They charged me with Eugene Anderson's murder, even though they knew I was in California. Matter of fact, I was in California as Jesse Jackson's bodyguard, so there wasn't any question about where I was. Anyhow, the Baltimore police ended up having to let everybody they charged go.

It really wasn't easy to hold it all together, to stay sane and keep things like the Free Breakfast Program going when all this sick stuff was going on. But most of the sick stuff was coming from the police.

I Was One of the People They Rolled Up

EDDIE: So we got rid of Warren Hart. And that's how I end up in the government files.

We didn't think the infiltrations stopped

117

with Warren. We knew people were being assassinated and framed and set up. We knew the local and the state police had informers in our midst. What we didn't know was that the NSA was involved, because it was basically an invisible agency. It turned out the National Security Agency had the largest spy apparatus in the world.[4]

At that time, though, you couldn't separate the NSA's efforts from the FBI's Counterintelligence Program. Everybody thinks it was just COINTELPRO, but the different surveillance agencies were infiltrating and snitching on each other, turning people against each other.

Stokely Carmichael almost got killed. Some agent put a CIA report form with Stokely's "signature" and information on it in another Panther's car that Stokely had been riding in. The owner comes back to his car and, as he gets in, he sees this paper on the seat where Stokely was sitting. He pulls it out and says, "Oh, a CIA report."

Of course he calls the Party office, so they send a team from California to investigate. But this is big; this is Stokely Carmichael, who's a field marshal. You don't accuse him unless you got some real stuff there.

Meanwhile, the FBI calls Stokely's mother and says, "The Panthers are coming to kill your son." She calls Stokely and says, "I got a warning from the FBI that the Panthers think you're a CIA informer. They say you're going to get killed. You got to get out of town." Stokely Carmichael bought an airline ticket that night and went to Africa.

It was twenty years before he came back. The government was doing this, time and time again. When one agent became suspect they would point a finger at another agent.

So they rolled us up. Of course, I was one of the people they rolled up. After a while, there was no leaders left. In some cases, like New York, New Jersey, Pennsylvania, the remaining Panthers went underground and formed the Black Liberation Army. That was a direct reaction to the attacks on all the chapters.

The government was satisfied, because what they didn't want was organizing in communities. In Oakland, some stayed around to do the electoral politics thing, getting involved with mayoral campaigns and that stuff. But pretty much, they finished the Panthers, turned them against each other. That's what they did here in Maryland, and that's how we first got locked up.

I definitely see my own legal case as part

of the government onslaught against the Panthers. Oh yes.

CHAPTER 9:
WE'RE COOL, AND
FUCK WHAT THEY SAY

On the evening of April 24, 1970, two Baltimore City police officers, Donald Sager and Stanley Sierakowski, were called to the scene of a domestic disturbance in Baltimore's Upton neighborhood. Returning to their cars, they encountered gunfire that wounded Officer Sierakowski and killed Officer Sager. About an hour later, two African American men, Jack Ivory Johnson and Jackie Powell, were arrested near the scene. The same night, two other officers subsequently spotted a man who, when asked to stop, fled, then allegedly turned and fired back at police. Although it was dark, one of the officers, Roger Nolan, identified the shooter as known Panther leader, Marshall "Eddie" Conway.

On April 26, claiming that the Black Panther Party had set up the attack, police arrested Eddie at the downtown Baltimore Post Office on 111 N. Calvert Street, where he was working the night shift. Eddie was charged with organizing and ordering the shootings, later with being one of the shooters.

In addition to arresting Johnson and Powell, and then Eddie, police arrested at least six other Panthers, conflating this shooting case with the murder of Eugene Anderson, whose body had been found the previous October. Ultimately, the Anderson charges resulted in no lasting conviction.[1] Meanwhile, the prosecution zeroed in on Eddie Conway, separating him from his two codefendants and charging him with first-degree and attempted murder. Powell and Johnson were also charged with murder.

Nelson Kandel, Eddie's original defense attorney, wanted to pursue the case on nonpolitical grounds, and was fairly confident Eddie could beat the rather flimsy criminal charges. But Panther headquarters in Oakland wanted to use Eddie's case to expose the racism and injustice embedded in US law enforcement. This was the message that Paul conveyed to Eddie's team: a political defense was the one correct way for Eddie to proceed.

So Kandel was dismissed, and Eddie asked movement lawyers Charles Garry and William Kunstler, who had offered their services pro bono, to represent him. The court denied Eddie's request, instead appointing an attorney named James McAllister. Eddie asked for another attorney; McAllister was not replaced.

Suddenly, in court, Jack Johnson, who had agreed to bear witness against Eddie, backtracked and refused to testify, saying that police had beaten and intimidated him into giving his statement. Years after the fact, Paul Coates remembers Johnson's attorney,

> who I think was some kind of agent. He convinced him, along with some rough treatment from the police, to become a state's witness. Come time for trial, he came into court and renounced a confession he made, even though they told him he'd end up in jail for the rest of his life.

The prosecution, having neither direct evidence nor a direct eyewitness, realized it needed backup.[2] So from a Michigan jail, the State of Maryland procured one Charles Reynolds, who was serving time for passing bad checks, and moved him into Eddie Conway's cell in Baltimore. Recognizing Reynolds as a known police informant, Eddie vigorously protested the move, to no avail.

Reynolds, as the prosecution's new chief witness, gave testimony to replace the story Johnson had recanted. He claimed that Eddie had confessed the shootings to him, adding that Eddie had even stolen Sierakowski's watch. For his cooperation, Reynolds requested that the State of Maryland vouch for him at Michigan's parole board.

Eddie's trial began in January 1971. On March 3, he was convicted of murder in the first degree and two counts of assault with intent to murder. He received a life sentence for the killing of Officer Sager, to be followed — should he manage to outlive a life sentence — by fifteen years for the wounding of Officer Sierakowski and another fifteen years for shooting at Officer Nolan. Before Eddie's sentencing, Judge Charles D. Harris praised James McAllister's lawyering, even though Eddie had rejected McAllister as his attorney and had refused to participate with McAllister at his trial.[3]

Back in Oakland, the Panther Party offered more help, and Paul Coates went to Oakland to get it. If the Panthers had been aware of the full reach of COINTELPRO, Eddie and his codefendants might have received some real guidance. Instead, headquarters demanded that Paul abandon his imprisoned friends in Baltimore and give himself over to building the Panther Party on the West Coast. Paul refused, and for that, was expelled from the Party.

Years later, from prison, Eddie Conway

wrote a memoir describing how, in deploying sham prosecutions against Black militants, the government effectively replaced one time-tested form of judicial racism with another:

> The alleged murder of police officers would soon take the place of the mythological rape of white women as the basis for the legal lynching of Black men.[4]

Middle-Class Union Man to Jail

PAUL: Eddie's case affected me immediately. There was the shooting that went down, in 1970. The two folks arrested soon after were Jackie Powell and Jack Johnson. Then you were arrested.

EDDIE: Yeah, when I was at work. A police had been shot, killed, and another police had been shot and wounded, a third police had been shot at. They locked up several other Panthers. A couple of days later, they came and got me at the post office. Charged me at first with organizing and ordering it, and then with being a participant.

PAUL: The next morning at six o'clock, I get a call from the defense captain [John Clark, who had replaced Warren Hart]. He said, "Eddie's been arrested, get your ass down here. We got TE to move."

EDDIE: [*Laughing*] That's technical equipment. Which stands for weapons.

PAUL: Yeah. Now, this defense captain — I mean, he said this over the phone. I'm the only one with a car, so I picked him and a couple of other folks up, and we went over to the Panther house where the guns were.

There are no cops, no traffic — nothing around. We had to kick in the cellar window to get in the house — 'cause they hadn't brought the key. So we kick in the window, and we start taking guns out. On the third load of guns, the police are there. We're arrested. I get fifteen attempted murder charges — I don't know if you know that —

EDDIE: No, I did not know that.

PAUL: Yeah, fifteen attempted murder charges. Because I was the last person out of the house —

EDDIE: With an armful of guns —

PAUL: No, I had one rifle. I come out and I'm surrounded with police shotguns. This was 1970, after Fred [Hampton] got killed.

So I'm scared shitless. I'm thinking, "They're going to take me out." I think the only reason they didn't shoot me down was because I was totally surrounded by cops, I'm in this son-of-a-bitch semi-circle. If they'd started shooting, they would have shot each other, too. [*Laughing*] So that's why I got fifteen attempted murder charges, cause of all the cops.

At that time, I worked for United Airlines. That job was *gone* after I got arrested. So Eddie's arrest immediately changed my life. I went from a nice, middle-class, union man raising a family — to jail. That accelerated my politicization. It was my first arrest with the Panthers.

EDDIE: But you got out —

PAUL: I got out on bail, yeah. Let me think. Did they bust us again? Seems like we got busted for doing a demonstration of support around the jail. But they dropped all those charges. None of those guys that had the guns were convicted — the police just kept the guns. That was a classic case of draining the Panther bail fund. No charges came out of that for anybody.

EDDIE: I had a lawyer who advocated a

criminal defense, and that's what I should have done, but I knew I wasn't locked up for any criminal reason.

I didn't know I had a COINTELPRO file at that time. Back then, even though you'd hear that so-and-so's office had been blown up, so-and-so lieutenant got shot and killed, so-and-so's car disappeared with two people in it, it all seemed random, so I was still thinking my case was a local phenomenon. It just seemed like, "OK, we have to fight and we can probably win." I thought that all this shit ain't gonna stand up. How they gonna lock somebody up with no evidence, no witnesses, and keep him in jail? They can't do that. [*Laughs big*] Little did I know.

Obviously, they could do it — and did do it.

PAUL: But they never had a real case.

EDDIE: Inside jail, I saved a lot of people's lives, including the life of Charles Reynolds. He's the guy they put in my cell to inform on me. He was a known informant. But once I realized how dirty they were playing, I started calculating how to avoid the pitfalls.

When they put Charles Reynolds in my cell, the other Panthers wanted to jump him and beat him up. But I figured, OK, if he gets beat up, I'm going to get a conspiracy assault charge and then they'll really have something to hold me for. "Conway had this done." So I told people not to beat him up. After all, that was why they put Reynolds there in the first place.

I'm constantly trying to calculate how not to let them put us in a position where we can't get out. Eventually, everybody walked away except for two Panthers, Jack Johnson and Jack Powell. And then they glued me to this thing.

I still didn't think I would get convicted. Even though I seen what they did with the police informer. This is something I question now about my own naïveté. I'm like, "How can you do this to a person? What jury would go for this? There still has to be justice in America." I still can't figure out why —

PAUL: So the prosecution had Charles Reynolds. Part of Reynolds's story was that I had put Eddie up to it. According to him, I had told Eddie that, in order for Eddie to be a Panther, he had to kill a cop — that all Panthers had to kill a cop. According to Charles Reynolds, I'd given Eddie cough syrup on his birthday — cough syrup and marijuana — and sent him out to kill a cop. Of course, the flaw in that is I wasn't even in the Party at that time.

EDDIE: They wanted to lock Paul up, too. Then, during the trial, you were the defense captain, right?

PAUL: Yeah, at that time.

EDDIE: That's why they wanted to disrupt you.

PAUL: I don't know that that's so. I think they were more interested in substantiating a case against you, Eddie, 'cause they really didn't have anything against you. Initially, they thought they did, because Jack Johnson was going to testify for the prosecution, but Johnson recanted. So that left Nolan, the cop. He claimed that he knew you from the street. But he also claimed it was late at night, and he saw you a long distance away, mysteriously under a streetlight. That's the only testimony they had and, in Maryland, there had to be corroborating testimony.

So the prosecution went up to Detroit, where Charles Reynolds was in jail, to make the deal with Reynolds. I don't think it was about me.

You Can See the Tailfins

PAUL: For a while Eddie and I were in Baltimore City Jail together. That was where they sent us after we were busted with the guns.

You know, that bust is captured in the Stanley Nelson film, right? *The Black Panthers: Vanguard of the Revolution.* I didn't even realize there was footage. It's only about eleven seconds. I'm watching this film and when the narrator starts talking about the New York Panthers getting arrested, the footage shows some cops arresting Panthers.

I look at the footage and I say, "That don't look like New York." Because it had houses, not huge buildings. I say, "That looks more like Baltimore." Then I say, "Damn. That guy looks like Will Joiner." I look further and I say, "That *is* Will Joiner." I say, "That guy looks like me. That *is* me." I had no idea.

But it's less important that I was in the film, and more important that the cops would have had cameras on the scene to record that stuff. Which means they had this well orchestrated. So there I am, coming out of the house. I knew it was crazy, and I still did it. I'm coming out of the house with a gun.

After the bust, I saw photos in the [*Balti-*

131

more] *Sun* newspaper of me being placed in the car. But I didn't know anything about them having the arrest filmed. You know the other thing I remember? Back when I got arrested, I felt so defiant. I saw myself as this big, proud Black Panther. But in that film clip, you see a dejected Paul Coates with his head down. [*Laughs big, slapping table*] Like I'm saying to myself, "Damn. They got me. There goes my union job."

I had to play that clip over and over and over again. It's clearly us because my car, which we were loading the guns into, is there — you can see the tailfins. The tailfins are there.

Eddie Convicted: A Total Surprise

PAUL: I think Eddie and I really began working together after John Clark, our defense captain, was kidnapped.

EDDIE: Yeah, bounty hunters kidnapped the defense captain and snatched him away to California.

PAUL: And the Baltimore police actually assisted them. They put a circle of police officers around John one day as we came out of the courtroom after arraignment on the gun charges. The bail bondman steps into the middle of the circle pulling John in and says, "You're under arrest. I'm taking you back to California."

I'm thinking it's total bullshit. But the defense captain says, "OK, they got me." [*Eddie and Paul roar with laughter*]

EDDIE: I have no idea what that California case was, but he had jumped bail on it and they used that to bust up the Panthers.

PAUL: Once they kidnapped the defense captain, I became the person in charge of Baltimore. At that point, Eddie and I had to work together. We had to depend on each other.

EDDIE: Yeah. We had to trust each other.

PAUL: I'm communicating instructions half the time from California, the other half of the damn time, he and I are making it up. Because California was, for the largest part, nonresponsive. Just nonresponsive.

EDDIE: I think they were overwhelmed.

PAUL: He's being kind.

EDDIE: I might be. But there was the case

up in New Haven going on at the time. There was the Panther 21 case in New York; stuff down in New Orleans; Geronimo Pratt was being ran to ground; Huey was hiding up in the penthouse. It was really a system overload.[5] And when Des Moines blew up, it was just too much.

PAUL: Once Eddie was arrested, we wanted him released, but our thing at the time was pointing out contradictions in the system. We saw him coming out; the people rising up. There would be revolution, you know what I mean?

Initially, there was that lawyer on the case, Nelson Kandel, who felt that Eddie could beat the criminal charges. But our instructions from California were that this is a political case, so they were going to send a political lawyer to try it. That's the shit we went for.

EDDIE: Yeah, we were both behind that. For one thing, it was clear that it was a political case. It *was* a frame-up. If we played by the regular rules, we were going to end up hanging — I mean literally, they were attempting to kill me. So we thought if we have to fight, at least let's fight with people whose political perspective we trust.

PAUL: That's pretty much the way we approached it. When Kandel wanted to deal with this as a criminal case, it was me that communicated with the Panther leadership in California, and it was me who brought back, "No, we're not going with Kandel. We're going to wait for political lawyers." I've always carried a — I'll go with it as *guilt*. Because I'm the person who carried the message from Central Headquarters to Eddie that this was going to be dealt with as a political case.

After Eddie's conviction, the Panthers called me to California. So I went, thinking that we were going to discuss the political prisoners. But they didn't give a shit about these guys being in jail. That's one of the saddest — it's hard to say this. When I got to California, what I encountered — from the same person who put me in charge of the Baltimore chapter — was, "Coates, now we got your ass out here, we're going to break you." That's the kind of time they were on; they were focused on breaking my attachment to Baltimore, which was the people in jail. We still had at least three people inside, and other people under charges at that time. And nary a conversation about it. I reached a point where I said, "I don't know what's going to happen, but

135

I got to go."

EDDIE: And I'm seeing this from a cell, under the pressure of a traumatic life change, and getting everything secondhand. I did not know the dynamics or the logistics of what was going on.

PAUL: See, Huey had come up with this program to politically take over Oakland. Bobby [Seale] was going to run for mayor. It made no sense to me and many other people that you would close down the local Panther chapters and move all those Panthers across the country to Oakland. But it made sense to them because they were California-centric.

EDDIE: And Chinese-centric. Where that came from is Mao, the Long March. Back to a liberated base area, you gain control of that area and then move back out strategically to the next area and the next. That was part of the *Red Book* and Huey's trip to China. Like, "We're under attack, let's do the Long March." The Long March was taking Paul and the other chapters back to California.

PAUL: You have to understand, to people on

the East Coast, California was our Mecca. Everybody wanted to go to California. And then when you actually went there and you saw: WHOA — what is this about? Then they expelled me from the Party.

When you're expelled, you can't have any contact with other Party people. For Eddie to have contact with me would mean that he risked expulsion, you see? That was a choice he had to make. So I went to see him and I told him that I was out of the Party. My commitment was to come back — because I clearly wasn't leaving him. I wasn't leaving any of them in jail. So I think our long-term commitment began with Eddie and me deciding that we were cool — and basically fuck what they say in the Party. Jack Johnson also said fuck them. So did Jackie Powell. We began working immediately. Immediately.

EDDIE: Part of me had decided I was going to be convicted and executed, so I basically had not participated in the trial. When the verdict came back with life and thirty years, and not the execution part, I was relieved. By then I had given up on the criminal justice system. I'd been there and beyond.

PAUL: I never felt Eddie was going to be

137

convicted. It was a total surprise. Total surprise. Especially because our lawyer felt it was a weak case and the information was shaky. They had a forced confession from Jack Johnson they weren't even sure they could use, and we felt that we could demolish that. They had a jail-cell informant, who was their strongest evidence. Who's going to believe that shit? I thought our case was good. I still feel that way.

EDDIE: We made that mistake based on ideology, our belief that we were going to fight to the death. I was as supportive of a political trial as California was. But perhaps the entire movement of that period made a critical error in thinking this was our time. We'd fight and die if we needed to. Bring it — you know?

PAUL: I don't remember that we went to any elders for advice about this. I don't know that we would have listened to the elders —

EDDIE: Yeah, because unfortunately, we had written the elders off. Either they were from the civil rights movement, or the more radical communist movement. They were sellouts, over thirty. Their advice wouldn't have resonated with us.

PAUL: But inside of feeling that guilt thing, I am not *guilty.* There's no way I could have known at the time.

EDDIE: We were in the moment, and that's what the climate dictated. But Paul was always the main person on our defense committee, through all those years. From the very first committee that was established by a network of Panthers and Panther supporters. I think Paul and I knew each other better and better because of the case. Because Paul hung in there.

These Cats Were My Responsibility
PAUL: I think my relationship with Eddie became cemented when I came back from Oakland. Going to visit him, he had to make a choice between whether he was going to obey the edicts of the Panther Party or whether he would trust that I was going to be his eyes and his ears. At that point he could have said, "Look man, I don't want nothing to do with you; I'm cool with the Panthers." But he didn't. That may have been one of the great markers in our relationship. It was a moment for me that I began really liking Eddie.

What I truly liked about Eddie was that he was not crazy in the jail or inciting other people to craziness. That he was still honoring the principles of the Panther Party. And that he didn't crumble under the pressure of jail, he was still manly. Those were things I could admire.

Truly, there is some remorse. But it wasn't like I walked around every day saying, "Oh shit, let me thrash myself one more time." I went for the okey-doke. I accepted, "Okey-doke, the Party got this covered. Let's focus on making Eddie's case political, and the Party will have lawyers come in . . ." Yeah, there is some remorse with that.

I don't know how it colored my relationship with Eddie. Let's just say it was always present. It wasn't the controlling factor but it certainly was an anchor. It's not that I put Eddie in jail. But Eddie was someone I made a commitment to, and leaving him was unthinkable. He could trust me because of that, not because of the guilt. The guilt was my personal thing. See, those cats in jail were my responsibility, like it or not.

That kind of commitment is important. It comes up over and over again and it's ground zero for my relationships. It's not like I never fuck up, but first of all, I'm military. So if you and I are in this thing together and you tell me you got my back covered, I'm not worried about my back. And you don't worry; I got your back. It's just basic honesty. That shows up in my life and I still live inside of that.

CHAPTER 10:
LIFE PLUS THIRTY YEARS

The food in prison vending machines sucks. That's what you joke about. Machine-masticated squares of irradiated chicken, sprinkled with crumbs you hope come from some edible substance, and enclosed in two tasteless white buns slathered with industrial mayo. Energy drinks the color of antifreeze. Coffee not unlike muddy creek water . . . You buy this for yourself and for the person you're visiting. All this costs money. You laugh about spending thirty bucks on this stuff. Unless, of course, the prison you are visiting doesn't allow vending machines.

Then there's the cost of getting to the prison, hundreds, sometimes thousands of miles away. Cars, planes, busses, taxis, trains: you're willing to use them all, if you can afford them. You get there tired.

You get there early, maybe before 8:00 a.m., stand in line with other tired, hopeful visitors, waiting to spend your allotted time that day with the person you know who's held inside. You remove your shoes, belt, anything metal, give yourself up for inspection. The prison staff search and photograph you, and, if you pass, they stamp your hand with ultraviolet "security" ink. You leave behind clothing extras such as jackets or scarves or hats. You can't take anything in with you except your ID and some money for the vending machines.

This makes sense because the person you've come to visit has been judged dangerous. You, yourself, desiring contact with this person, may also be dangerous.

You comply. In the unyielding fight against crime, you agree to become a suspect. You agree to everything, because you want to reach this person, so much depends on this. Because you know this person you're about to see is suffering.

Of course, you'll never fully understand just how he or she suffers. After all, you yourself are not locked away from cars and cats and babies and sex and new clothes and on-the-street "hey-there's" and elections and computers and Facebook and the latest food fads. You live with the reality that this person has borne, and will continue to bear, hours, days, years, sealed away from the mixed blessings that we call life outside. Taken, it seems, from the Earth itself, to a world where one's identity redounds to that of legal property, to that of an enslaved being.

And while you yourself may not be an innately happy person, you want to bring the person you're visiting some happiness. News, gossip, stories you embellish from your own life. You want to bring hope — which is all of that and more. Throughout this visit, your subconscious will silently tabulate and assess just how your individual hearts are broken, compare the unbridgeable differences between you. This is, of course, something you will never discuss. You won't come much closer than, "You OK? They treating you right?"

Everyone who regularly goes to see people inside prison has, of course, their own take on the experience, but I do believe this is a common routine for a "contact" visit. Along with higher-security visits through Plexiglas walls, it's the kind of routine that millions go through every day in the United States to spend a little monitored time with people they love and respect. It's the kind of routine Paul Coates went through for years, to have Eddie's back.

As Eddie began a life locked away from the hopeful tumult of a world he'd been trying to fix, Paul Coates moved on, but not away. The war in Vietnam ended; other proxy wars were to begin. The Panther Party, the Black Liberation Army, then other militant leftist organizations were crushed or simply ceased to exist. More Black people were shot down in the street, or in their homes. Prisons filled, then overfilled. More children were born into Paul's family; Eddie gradually lost touch with his son, Ronald. One day, Eddie's father arrived at the prison to tell him that, though he loved Eddie, he couldn't visit him ever again: "[H]e could not bear the weight that came with walking into that place."[1]

And Paul kept coming to visit Eddie. Here are Paul and Eddie, talking about their lives through the 1970s, the 1980s, the 1990s, and on into the first years of twenty-first century.

I Didn't Want to See a Dude

EDDIE: I spent forty-four years, from 1970 until 2014, in the prison system. In all the various different levels of incarceration.

I think probably the first month or two, I was in a state of disbelief. My initial reaction was that I'm not getting caught up in prison politics and prison organizing. I needed to be focused on how to get me back outside, because I felt separated from the community. But when I got into the prison system, there were a hundred potential revolutionaries there, all of them clamoring, "Help, help, we've been waiting. Why did it take you so long to get here?"

At first, I resisted. But some of them were so sincere that it made me say, "OK, I have some ideas, some skills they could use." So I got sucked into the prison movement. Before I know it, we were working to make changes in the prison. And it turned out I never felt separated from the community because the work we did inside kept us attached to the community. We brought the community, the support base, into the prison environment.

The first thing I saw when I walked in the place was birds flying overhead inside the building. We're ducking bird crap, the windows are broke out, there's draconian behavior by the guards. They'd just snatch somebody and start beating them and drag them through the whole shop, take them out front and dump them in the parking lot and then look back at us and say, "Yeah. So what?" That hit my nerves. Right away I said, "OK we're going to change that."

We couldn't form a Panther chapter because Oakland had banned new chapters. So we started something called the Maryland Penitentiary Inter-Communal Survival Collective.[2] Everybody in the prison called us Panthers, but we never wanted them to call us that.

Initially, we organized to clean the prison up. We pushed and pushed and forced them to put in plastic windows. Because we couldn't do anything about the birds until the windows got in. Then we got the place de-birded, for want of a better word. Sanitized.

The overall thing was, "We need Black guards in here. Because y'all can't communicate and this is part of what the frustration and the violence is about."

We also started pushing for creature comforts. Like we realized we did not have a library so we pushed for a library. There was maybe two TVs for four hundred people. That was the source of all kinds of violence. Because you've got a hundred people sitting there watching something and Joe might come up with ten people and say, "We want to watch the fight," or "We want to watch Judy shake her booty." So in order to get around that conflict, we needed to get people their own TVs.

Then we created a survival program for people on lockup [solitary]. We developed the ability to look out for people that got arbitrarily snatched up by the guards and didn't have anything, no soap, no toothpaste, no shaving equipment, that kind of stuff. In fact, Rap Brown took advantage of it when he got locked up there.

For a minute, we also created a guerrilla radio program. Finally, we produced a paper, which was our newsletter inside. Matter of fact, the administration ended up starting an official newspaper to stop us from doing that.

My world shrunk down to the prison system. I used to see myself as national and international — all of a sudden, I become "prisoner." Prison became my whole world. Living in that world probably allowed me to survive, but it cut me off from the outside and family and relations. I had to shut all that stuff down to stay alive in that box. But I never got mad with people on the outside for not understanding.

This is something I do realize — I tend to ignore negativity. So I focused on the people that wanted to help, on people who were doing stuff. There was times when people maybe didn't step up the way I felt they should, but almost anybody was willing to help however they could. In some cases, maybe it was hot air, or they failed to reach their commitments. But there was always support from a wide range of people. I tried to dismiss the people I felt had let me down.

For instance, I worked with one particular guy in prison for six or seven years. He thought he was George Jackson reincarnated: black belt, martial artist, jungle fatigues — in fact, he was our karate instructor. Read all the books, knife in his mouth, the whole nine yards. Then he gets released.

They open the door — he walked *through* that door, took off his jungle fatigues; he threw the *Red Book* on the penitentiary steps. The next time we seen him, two weeks later, he had a Jheri curl, a maxi leather coat, two sex workers, and a pimpmobile.

Him and I had been in the trenches — life and death trenches. And in the space of a door, he just changed. That was devastating. Because my life was in his hands and his life was in my hands for years. It was not a fantasy; it was real life and death situations. And there he is, pimping. So I have to say, "OK, I can't be attached to people," because there's going to be some who are going to fail, and if I get caught up like that, *I'm* going to fail.

But win or lose, Paul was just there for whatever we needed. Black Classic Press that exists today grew out of the fact that we needed to get political books to prisoners. Paul was outside sending books to people inside, and that led to him getting a bookstore. I think we named our project the George Jackson Prison Movement. After he got a bookstore, it was like, "Shit, we could print some of these books." So we talked about getting a press.

Paul would come to see me, although I was on lockup quite a bit in solitary confinement. But I also saw lawyers and visitors. I could probably only allow Paul to visit me like once a month, because there were so many people I wanted to see, and you only get so many visits. Also, Paul was a dude. I didn't want to see a dude. [*Laughs big*] But I seen him whenever I needed to see him.

What do I remember missing most about the outside world? [*Long pause*] Sex. Yeah, pretty much.

Juche and the Black Book

PAUL: While I was with the Panther Party, publishing wasn't an aspiration at all. Publishing came out of searching for a way to fight for Eddie Conway. It was for Eddie more that than anything. The Panthers were enamored of Kim Il-Sung, the North Korean leader, so we used to read his works. When Eldridge Cleaver was in North Korea, he was part of what influenced us to do that reading. The concept of Juche [self-reliance] was very big.

There was this one story to explain Juche and inspire the troops. Some leader asks a battalion of soldiers, "What is the most powerful weapon you go into combat with?" The first soldier says, "A rifle. With a rifle, I can kill lots of the enemy." And the leader says, "Cool." And turns to the next guy. "What about you?" The next guy says, "A grenade. With a grenade I can kill more." Somebody else ramps up and says "Artillery," or something like that.

Then the commander goes to this strongest soldier and he says, "All of that's good — but a mimeograph machine is best." This one soldier sacrificed all in this story to save a mimeograph machine. Because, with the mimeograph machine, he could kill the consciousness — he could kill the will of opposing armies. With propaganda. You with me there? I still remember that very well. For me, it was a story of how powerful the printing press was. And we did have a press in the Baltimore chapter.

One time, I was responsible for working with the National Committee to Combat Fascism. They had an office in DC with one of the best printing operations in the country. They had presses, and they would produce pamphlets and posters. The power and the ability to use the press was alive in my consciousness when I left the Panther Party.

To get books into Eddie's prison, we started off as the George Jackson Prison Movement. From that came a bookstore called The Black Book, which I started in 1972. Eddie was in jail but I consulted with him the whole time. We felt we could work together, establishing this bookstore that could allow the people on the inside to work. Eddie organized the guys on the inside to receive the books. He was excited about it, because it gave them something concrete and positive to do in the joint.

Eddie and I also planned a publishing house that would supply books to The Black Book and other bookstores. It would publish books for people in the United States and around the world, as long as they dealt with struggle. Original manuscripts. People would write anything that dealt with fighting ignorance and killing the mind of the enemy. We weren't considering reprinting at that time; the idea of reprinting and Black Classic Press came later.

So outside the jail, I was organizing the bookstore with about six or seven of us, I can't remember. We were all "exes," like ex-Panthers, ex-socialists, ex-what-have-you's.

Bottom line is, we couldn't agree on anything.

There were some Detroit revolutionary movement folks. There was myself and another brother from the Panther Party, Reginald Howard. There were one or two Black nationalists, and all of us were working through our pasts. I came up with the platform and program for the George Jackson Prison Movement — which was one thing we could agree on, working with people in jail. This goes back to Juche — because we organized around books.

It wasn't much of a movement, because after only a few weeks, the other guys went away. We had finally all agreed. They said, "A bookstore! That's a good idea!" Then they said, "Bye, *you* do it." That's exactly what happened. [*Laughs*]

The Black Book was first located at 1609 Pennsylvania Avenue, in Baltimore. Setting up the store, we had one event. I arranged with Eddie to do a book drive. We were going to have a crab feast and book party at some church, where people were supposed to bring used books. We were selling tickets, but most of the outside crew didn't sell any; they just disappeared.

So when I say "we," it was mainly myself and Reginald Howard. Howard, as we called him, died in 2010. A number of bad things happened and he actually went crazy. He was on the streets here for years. We used to hook up, and we'd talk. He would give me the wisdom of staying on the street and how logical that was.

The George Jackson Prison Movement, the bookstore, the publishing company, the printing press — all of that was connected to prison work. We were supposed to get books into the jail. You see, I believe that some of our best minds, some of our best people, are in jail. Some of the people we need to help us.

The Human Fly Incident

EDDIE: Back when I went into the prison system, there was developing a strong community involvement in prisons, rehabilitation, etcetera. People went to prison mainly for various criminal violations. And then people with politics started going in — white, Black, Latino, Puerto Rican, Native American political prisoners.

Prisoners started getting organized, challenging the inhumane. You had Attica in New York, where the prison exploded. White and Black prisoners, they got together; they took over the prison. On the West Coast, there was a form of retaliation for the murders of prisoners. George Jackson is probably the highest symbol of resistance at that time.[3] Of course, ultimately, he was assassinated in the prison yard.

The one thing we recognized in the Maryland Penitentiary was the 13th Amendment, which says slavery is abolished in the United States except for people in prison, convicted of crimes. So we organized a United Labor Union for prisoners. We got labor unions outside involved; we got government officials, congresspeople involved. We pushed for minimum wage for prisoners.

At that time, probably around 1972, we were making something like nine cents an hour, turning out products for the state that was selling those products and making millions of dollars. So we figured we could start a labor union and get it recognized — 1199E was prepared to do that. That's the labor union Martin Luther King supported in Memphis, where he got assassinated.

We felt we could help these people stand up and demand their rights. The guards were always trying to make them think they were less than human, because they broke the law and society was punishing them. A union would also change how prisoners saw themselves. At the same time, we figured that if they had to pay every prisoner minimum wage, states would stop incarcerating people, because the labor would no longer be so cheap. We knew we probably weren't going to get a real salary, but we were going to shut the whole prison system down and set an example. If we could do that, then there would be no economic incentive in incarcerating people from the Black population.

Now, the response to Attica was very violent; the response to George Jackson was very violent. But what we didn't understand was that the response to organizing a labor union was going to be way more complicated. The prison administration began to create conflicts inside the prison.

Because the people organizing the labor union were political activists, the first thing the administrators told the prison population was, "Communists are taking over. They want to run the jail. They're against the American way of life."

But we went ahead and organized. We signed up enough people. We prevented any kind of violence — because the administration kept trying to create violence in the population so they would have an excuse to shut it down. We wouldn't let anybody get in fights; there was no incidents. We did all the paperwork, the charter, the articles.

We also had outside support. There was Parren Mitchell, who had just become the first Black person from Maryland elected to Congress; there was Kitty Broady, a top radio personality; there was Fred Punch, an organizer and 1199E president; there was Paul Coates, a key outside advisor; and there was another person — oh, the owner of the Arena Players theater in Baltimore. So we were at the point when all we had to do was to be accepted outside by 1199E. [*Big laugh*]

That union thing didn't work out well.

There was a midnight raid. They used this thing called the Human Fly Incident.

Here's what happened. The penitentiary is probably five stories up. So they had about ten junkies — I mean guys that were actually on drugs — climb up the outside wall, through the prison windows. They climbed up the side — it's cement down on the ground, so if any one of them fell down, he was dead.

They used that incident to close the jail down. Plus, they did a midnight raid on us. The prison said that we had organized this Human Fly Incident, so the guards come around in the middle of the night and lock all our leaders up. Then, after they got all the junkies down and shook them out, they

157

announced that the junkies did that in support of the union. Which was the most ludicrous thing ever.

They said, "The outside people were the ones that made this happen. They're agitators." They blamed Paul and all these prominent people in the city, in the state, for inciting us. And they put us prisoners on lockdown, so there wasn't nothing we could do or say about it.

There was nothing the outside 1199E union could do about it, either, because they were accused of instigating. No prison had ever organized a union before. This was virgin territory, and it could have went either way. Of course, it went the way the prison directed it.[4]

Past Route 175 Where the Jail Was

PAUL: I took all my kids to visit Eddie. Like my father, I would keep my kids with me, so if I happened to have them in the car and I was going to the jail, then they were going too. I can't speak for the kids about what those visits were like. I don't know how many of them keep those memories. Later, I took one of my grandsons in to see Eddie. I still have a picture of one of them with me and Eddie because you know how

158

important those photos you take in prison are.[5]

Sometimes Eddie would share what was going on with him and what was bothering him that he couldn't control, and there were times I would do the same. It was exciting if Eddie had some legal stuff going on and there was hope for him getting out, or if something was happening in the wider social world that brought our spirits up. But when his legal case wasn't going well, it could get real depressing.

Basically I was Eddie's legal adviser, his personal adviser, and his brother, all rolled up into one. I was his confidant on those issues that he considered sensitive enough to share. Most of the time I was not involved in Eddie's political campaigns; that was his domain. He and I came to that conclusion early on. Consequently, that allowed him to work with a lot of other, different people. They would have burnt me out — I couldn't take all those people.

Did we argue about stuff? We bonded on most things. He understood the vision for Black Classic Press. I understood the political things he was doing. The only thing we disagreed on was the extent that he would allow people to call him a political prisoner. My thought was that "political prisoner" didn't serve any purpose for him. For me, the focus was that Eddie was unjustly imprisoned. That became something we could build a case around. He agreed with that, but when he wrote his book [*Marshall Law*], he described himself as a political prisoner. But that really was his call; he was the one doing the time.

Eddie made up at least half of my whole life while he was in prison. It would vary from time to time, but he never took up less than 50 percent. Sometimes it would be more. You can see that if you understand that the Panther Party has never left me. If someone comes up to me and says, "I heard you were in the Panthers," Eddie's going to be present. How can I think about the Panther Party without thinking about him? Yeah, he's always there.

So our relationship was very close. And remains that way. For us, it was always a matter of me and Eddie, and then the world. Like, Eddie might have relationships with other political people, but those relationships were not going to go over top of ours. That was an unspoken bond between us. If you strip away the politics — take all that off the table — I would still end up with a brother who's a good man. A man who's a good thinker, who wants justice in the world, and who lives that way. He doesn't live inside of "who-am-I-going-to-cheat-tomorrow?" I should say, *if* you could strip all that away. The part I could never strip away was him wasting his life in jail. I couldn't do that.

So if I was driving home, past Route 175 where the jail was, I would always have to look in that direction. As I passed, I might say, "Should I go to the jail? Should I stop this evening?" And then, of course, the whole world would come up.

We Might Just Take Over the Prison

EDDIE: Initially, I couldn't call Paul. There were no phones. The only way you could make a phone call was go and Tom to a lieutenant or a captain, who would then ask you to inform on who's doing what in the jail. So very few people made phone calls. The exception was, "My mom is sick," or "Junior's in trouble and I need to straighten it out." But other than that, you didn't ask for a phone call.

After 1976 or '77, we forced them to put phones in, and I could call. I think we were probably able to get the phones because we had about three riots.

Sometimes, instead of riot, we might just take over the prison. Everybody be out in the yard, and demand to see the warden, refuse to go in, and stare down the guns until somebody comes out and negotiates with us. Of course, we challenged them on the legal front as well as in the yard. That's how we were able to affect almost everything.

We forced them to let us buy TVs. And all we had was uniforms, so we forced them to let us wear our street clothes. We forced them to hire Black police — which is still a mistake. [*Laughs*] We were thinking, "All these police are white, we need to have some brothers and sisters up in here." Then the Black cops were beating us worse than the white police, in some cases.

The prison gave in because that was the only way they could have peace. They never called in the state troopers — well, once they did. That time it really got out of hand.

What happened, it started as an escape attempt that went bad. Some guys tried to saw through the bars in the windows. They got discovered, but they were able to let people out of their cells, and there was an internal riot. That was the time they called in the state troopers.

They surrounded the penitentiary and closed everything down. At some point the cops used shotguns, blew in the doors, turned the dogs loose. Prisoners were barricaded up on the floor, ready to fight. It was bad.

Then some of the prisoners snatched up the police. There were people inside who had said things like, "If there's ever a riot, I'm gonna get that guard, Bill. Oh, there's Bill — you motherfucker." They actually tried to hang a couple of police, and other prisoners — some of them gangsters — saved the cops. Some prisoners dressed a couple of guards up in dresses and shit. It was terrible, terrible.

Riots are not something anybody wants in prison. Prisoners don't want riots because all kinds of behavior take place. Plus, stuff gets broken and never gets fixed. The cops say, "Well, you broke it."

You Going to Fear Me

PAUL: In his book, *The Beautiful Struggle,* Ta-Nehisi calls me a "practicing fascist." You know, that book started out as a biography of me. But as I read it, as his editor and agent read it, we all agreed his strongest writing was about him. The writing about me was like a Mack truck, but when he started talking about his experiences, it was like a Lamborghini, it was just so beautiful. So it became clear that his book was about

163

him, and his journey to manhood. But Ta-Nehisi's right about me. I was the enforcer in my house.

I had seven children by four different mothers and I wanted my kids together whenever possible. So yeah, in many ways I was this enforcer guy. I was the enforcer for Cheryl; I was the enforcer for Linda. If the kids had to be disciplined it fell to me. "I'll let your father deal with that when he gets in." I didn't have to be the enforcer so much for Patsy or Sola, because they had different family structures around them. But if the kids were with me I was that guy.

Here's the lineup. My children are Kelley, Kris, Bill, who later chose an African name, Damani. Then there's Malik, Johnathan, Ta-Nehisi, and Menelik. Most of them graduated from Howard. Malik graduated from Rensselaer. John graduated from Purdue. All of them are solidly based in education. Ta-Nehisi's the only one that didn't graduate from college, go figure.

Finding words for them is hard. Because I keep coming away with beautiful. All of my kids are just beautiful kids and they radiate in different ways. Most of my kids have values that may reflect some part of mine. Ta-Nehisi is politically close to his dad, but on his own terms and in his own way. He's challenging the world, he's looking at the world, seeing himself connected to his ancestral history.

Actually, not so much the girls, but all the boys, I think, came out of this space of not wanting to be their dad. I didn't want to be my dad, either. But my kids have values that are daddy-ish, you know. In *The Beautiful Struggle,* Ta-Nehisi tells his son, Samori, "I grew up in a hard house." I just say, "Well, Shorty, you don't know hard." Cause my father was hard. He was a hard man.

When my kids were young I would say, Here's the deal: It's either me or the street. That's all there is, there's no in-between. And hell yeah, you going to fear me. For me, that's the reality, particularly for young Black men. As I saw it, my job was to get them through.

They were confronted by so many threats. All Black kids are, but especially boys. The largest threat was the police. It really was my fear that if you screwed up, there's no one but the police. You act up in school; they're going to call the cops. You're dead; you're in jail; you've got a history. That is real today too. Because when you're out on the street, you got to think about bringing your ass home.

As your father, I don't know that I'm going to say the right thing all the time, but I know I'm going to say the best deliberative thing I can. I will have thought about it. In my house, you're not bringing women here; this is not a hangout; this is not a place for you to drink; this is not a place for you to get high. And if you say, fuck me? You need to go to the street. And if the street calls you — you can leave any time you want. Over on this side, this is not a democracy. I had and still do have three hard and fast rules.

The first is, you don't disrespect your elders. I would probably grab one of my kids today if I caught them disrespecting an elder in the street. If you disrespect elders then you have absolutely no concern about anyone else. The next thing is, you don't go to school and fuck up. I'm not talking academically; you do not confront teachers or administrators and threaten them. I'm not going to be that parent that jumps in and says, "My kid didn't do anything, and who are you, Miss Teacher?"

The third thing is, you will never disrespect your mother. I don't give a shit about sexism. What I know is your mother birthed you. Your mother wiped shit off your ass; she nursed you and gave to you. And because you're bigger than her, you're disrespecting her? Nothing is lower to me. Because if you do that to her, then you'll disrespect any woman. See, as a man I feel I can deal with your disrespect. You want to disrespect me? Let's go at it. Now, you can hate me, but my job is to get you across the line, and these are my rules. That's it.

I think Ta-Nehisi calling me a practicing fascist is pretty accurate. Again, it empowered me to get them through. But, to be honest with you, I don't know what else I could have done it with seven kids, five being boys. I think about it all the time. Five boys and two girls — and my job is to get you across the line. That's my side of it. Ta-Nehisi's might be different. As far as I'm concerned, he's fully entitled to share that.

I just did the best I could do. I always tried to deal with him and all my kids honestly, never lying. Ta-Nehisi's had to learn with his own son, Samori. But with one child, you got the luxury to work in all different kinds of ways.

The beautiful thing is, I have my grandkids now. I'm still concerned with how I'm going to get them across. And, like with my kids, I sometimes have the grandkids help out at the press.

I was just saying to Ta-Nehisi about my grandkids, "Man, these cats are real workers — I got happy workers here, right?" [*Laughing*] I know that's the side they show me. Because their parents tell me they be talking about me cold up behind my back.

Was I successful? I guess. I can only tell you that my greatest thing is getting my children through. I got my sons through. I got 'em through. Now what happens after today, I don't know. The fact is, I got results. Not without their mothers, I got to get that in. Their mothers gave me my children and my life, I want you to understand. [*Laughing*] I didn't — couldn't — get them through without their mothers.

He Feeds the Geese

EDDIE: In 1970 when I went in prison, no Black person thought their life expectancy was less than thirty years. Every Black person you met thought, "Oh, I'm going to be seventy" — even with the influx of drugs from Vietnam. I'm remembering a massive flood of heroin — the whole *Superfly* thing — that got out of control. But that fatalism wasn't there then.

Young people started developing that fatalism around the mid-'80s with the AIDS epidemic, and then with crack cocaine came the surge in violence. They were growing up and seeing their friends getting killed. They

168

were seeing their cousin, or somebody they knew get shot in the heart. They started thinking, "I'm going to do whatever I want, because I'm not going to get any older than twenty-five." They started to come to prison like that. "I don't care, shit, everybody I know is dead."

People disappear out of their lives. Joe up the street, all of a sudden, he don't come home anymore. He's in the penitentiary, or he's in Florida on the run. Whether they die or get taken away, they start disappearing. And somewhere in the '80s, when new drugs became prevalent, the morality changed among young people. The morality I grew up with is that you shouldn't hit a woman, you definitely don't hit your mother, but you damn sure never hit your grandmother.

One of the things I worked in then was a ten-week counseling program that encouraged people to get their lives together. So I was counseling, and the young guys were coming in, talking about how they beat the shit out of their grandmother or they kicked her down the steps because she flushed their drugs down the toilet. I could no longer work with people like that.

The thing about counseling is, the people you're talking to have got to feel that you have their interest at heart, that you like them and want the best for them. They have to have that sense. So I'm setting in front of these guys and I'm thinking, "Oh, if I could catch you alone in the back, I would . . ." [*makes teeth-bared, seething face*]. They could feel that. So I realized that I could no longer counsel. That stuff don't work if people aren't trying to change.

I had to step away from counseling for maybe twenty years. I worked in other programs, like the Seven Steps program,[6] I worked on the National Black Independent Party,[7] in the '80s. We also organized literacy programs. I was in charge of the penitentiary library, and so we used the library to organize. Famous Amos, the cookie thing? We were working with him.[8] It didn't have a name, it was just a literacy program. I organized GED classes, all kinds of activities. Not counseling.

But all during our organizing young people, the prison administration was also organizing them. The prison started giving them drugs and telling them that they should convince the other young people in the population not to participate in the activities we were encouraging.

There were some gangs then out in LA, some gangs in Chicago, in New York. But the gangs that we recognize now started off in the prison system, nurtured by the guards and the prison officials, allowed to grow in opposition to the political organizing that was going on. The guards encouraged the gangs, encouraged the drugs, to stop political people from gaining control of the prison populations. Those gangs caused a lot of violence, a lot of people died as a result. This is a part of prison you don't see.

The end result is the violence we are watching in the cities. Nobody talks about this. Everybody wonders, "Why is there so much murder? Why is this happening in poor and Black communities and communities of color? All of a sudden it's just bodies dropping."

In Baltimore, in particular, bodies are dropping every day. In Chicago, Newark, across the land. Of course, we can turn to Frantz Fanon's *Wretched of the Earth*, where he talks about the rage and the internal frustration of the oppressed. At some point, we lash out against the people around us, nearest us, blaming them for our oppression.

There's an ultra-maximum-security jail in Cumberland, Maryland. There are several high-security jails in Hagerstown. There is a high-security complex of jails in Eastern Shore. These jails are anywhere from seventy-five to 150 miles away from the urban centers, where most of the prison populations come from. What's unique about this is that the guard force is in those rural areas. They gained employment by working in those prisons after the industries left. Factories went to China, India, Mexico, and those people remained, without jobs.

Then the government built prisons. The Black people that lost their jobs in the urban areas were incarcerated in those prisons. Those Black populations came in conflict — cultural, racial, economic conflict — with the guard forces. There's constant battles going on, in Cumberland, Hagerstown, Eastern Shore.

Newspapers in the state have reported percentages of the guard force in these areas were Ku Klux Klan. In Cumberland, in particular, some guards belong to the National Guard unit from Western Maryland, West Virginia, and Western Pennsylvania. That National Guard unit was activated during the Iraq War.

When they went to Iraq, they were put in charge of the prisons there. They went to prisons like Abu Ghraib, where guards abused the Muslim prisoners, took their clothes off, disrespected them for their particular religious beliefs, put dogs on them. After that, the army brought them back. People from that same unit run the prisons up in Cumberland. Those people, when they're not in the National Guard, are working in the prison system. When they're back in the National Guard, for one weekend a month or so, they're learning how to handle prisoners.

I'm not saying the whole unit, en masse, but the same people. When they got back from Iraq, they continued that behavior with the prisoners, who were 75 percent or 80 percent Black. That particular guard force is probably 99 percent white.[9]

These prisoners are the lowest income group, miles from their homes. Their families are poor, far away, and it's a hardship to go and visit. So these prisoners don't get many visits. They might get one a month.

What happens? The prison population feels isolated. And prisoners are abused, they're beat up. Some of them are killed. They don't have any way of reaching out. Their phones are often cut off; their communication is controlled. So there's a certain attitude that develops among young prisoners.

First is: "OK, I'm guilty" — I hear this all

the time — "I'm guilty, they caught me, I'm doing my time." But behind that is: "I'm not supposed to be beat up, abused, and gassed. I'm not supposed to be treated like this."

But because nobody is responding to what's happening inside these prisons, the prisoners think you on the outside are endorsing that behavior.

"They locked us up. The taxpayers are paying them. They doing these horrible things to us. Nobody's saying anything about it. It's us against the world."

The prisoner will rebel.

I'll give you one example. This is a guy I knew. He's taking a shower. Other people are in the shower too. The guard come by: "Everybody out the shower." The guys come out, wet, half-soaped.

This guy, he's taking a minute too long. He's finishing whatever he's doing. Out come the teargas — *SH-SH-SH-SH* — the whole shower is sprayed. If you've ever been shot with teargas, you know how it affects you. Everybody in the area is sprayed.

This guy comes out, and he's mad. The next time something happens, he bucks. He gets beat up, he gets put in the hole. Eventually, he says, "OK, I can't win." He's mad, he's frustrated.

What I'm saying to you I've witnessed with my own eyes.

Then this man is walking in the yard somewhere. There's geese all over, around the yard — which is not normal; they should be flying South or something. Anyhow, he takes a slice of bread out of his pocket, and he feeds the geese, because that's how he is.

A guard sees him do it and stops him. Sends somebody to get a loaf of bread. And make him eat that loaf of bread. Because he fed the geese, he's got to eat the whole loaf.

But other prisoners are walking by — he's dehumanized. He's angry. He's standing there and he's going to eat that bread and if he doesn't, he's going to go into one of those lockup cells. He don't want to go there, cause he'll be away from his buddies in the yard. So he's eating that bread, but he's hating every moment of it, and he's feeling all this anger. These things build up, and at some point the prisoner says, "I can't do anything about this, I got to grit my teeth and just keep on going."

Then they let that guy out. But they don't just let him out. Every year, six hundred thousand prisoners are released.[10] In almost every state, those people who are released are angry.

Let's get back to this one guy. He's frustrated, he's been abused, and he gets on the street. He knows there was nothing he could do about what happened to him in there — but he's got this transferred aggression, rage, anger, it's all there. Then some misunderstanding happens, and you have a violent incident.

Maybe you have a guy from Eastern Shore or a guy from Cumberland, and they don't even know each other. They both got that anger. You have that explosion of violence. Inside, prisons are manufacturing the violence that we see in our community. People don't understand that; they're still asking, "Why is all this killing going on?"

This killing is going on because these thirteen- or fifteen-, eighteen-year-olds who have gone to prison are now twenty or twenty-five or thirty and they're out. They explode. "I ain't letting you do this to me. Because now I can do something about it."

It's like Frantz Fanon: it's your buddy's fault that you're not free.

Understand This: Since Slavery

EDDIE: Prison actually encourages gangs to form. In Maryland, if you belong to the Black Guerrilla Family, there's a whole area in which those members are housed. You all become a unit, a tribe. People are put in there and they either join or they become victimized. If you make the guards angry, they take you from wherever you were and put you in the Black Guerrilla housing area or with the Bloods or the Crips or Murder Inc or DMS, the white gang. Two or three of you in there, with three hundred people that want to get you.

This is how they control the population and this is how they create killers. Because those people come back to the community and they kill. They kill because they're angry; they kill because they think we have abandoned them; they kill because they never got visits because people couldn't afford to visit them. Or because, when people did come visit them, the people themselves are criminalized. They're searched and degraded and made to feel like they're involved in some criminal activity.

Just now, in the state of Maryland, there's a ban on hugging your family at visits.[11] It's in some prisons; in others, it's not — the best I can tell is that it's unevenly applied. That means fathers and mothers can no longer pick up their children, you can't hug your brother or sister, a mother can't hug her son or daughter. This is designed not only to isolate, but to further dehumanize people. It diminishes you when your family comes in, and you can't even hug your mother.

I can't emphasize this enough — *this violence is manufactured in prisons all over the country.* It's not just an instance where the capitalist system is taking away its surplus labor, where marginal populations are obsolete because manufacturing is now automated. You have something now that's the foundation of fascism: fear. That fear you have when you walk down the street and you see three or four people coming toward you, and it's like, "Damn, what might happen?"

You have that fear, first, because of the multinational corporations that control most of the media; that control what you get in terms of news. They're billionaire operations, and they run on the concept: If it bleeds it leads. "Baby Killed!" — "Shoot-out!" — "Bodies Over There!" You get tons and tons of stories about threats to your security and your safety. They make you think: "Well, maybe the police have a right to do this. We need more police. Let them do whatever it takes."

So, what's happening? Six hundred thousand people coming out of the prison system every year. See, everybody talks about the two million or more people in prisons, about the five to seven million people under some kind of jurisdiction, whether on parole or probation or in the hole. But nobody considers that flood of people being released. All these angry people, abused in these faraway places by the clash of culture, economics, and race. People that are angry, frustrated, and can't get a job because they're felons.

"Ban the box" don't mean nothing when you can go on the Internet and see who's coming in for a job interview. So these folks can't get hired, and at some point, they lose the ability to take care of themselves, unless they somehow break the law. And once they do, it justifies the cycle again, because: "Oh yeah, he had a gun; he got caught; he had drugs." It perpetuates itself.

And you are terrorized. You in turn allow things to happen in your name that further aggravates those people pouring back into the system.

This allows the militarization of the police forces in America. To the point of tanks, to the point of automatic weapons, of all kinds of weapons you haven't even seen yet, sound cannons, water cannons. Weapons you're not prepared for, they're distributing from the federal government down throughout the municipalities, in the event that you at some point should collectively say, "We want to change the economic system, and maybe have some say-so on the XL pipeline or fracking or how immigrants are treated or whether people should have gender rights." That government militarization has been built into the system that's now creating the conditions you see in Black neighborhoods. It's expanding into other neighborhoods.

One thing I think is important is the transfer of wealth. That 2008 crash? The Black community lost 50 percent of its wealth[12] — wealth it had accumulated since slavery. Understand this: Since slavery. Half of the wealth that was accumulated by the collective Black community, from 1865, is gone in six years. The white community lost a serious proportion of its wealth, too. Where did the wealth go? To a small minority of people. That's something to consider, because at some point impoverished people are going to act out.

Black Classic Press: The *Pamphlets* Were the Books

PAUL: I'm not much of an activist. I don't know that I ever made the choice to be an activist. You just won't find much history of me leading demonstrations, even if I have.

Matter of fact, most people just knew me as this mild-mannered guy that came to the joint to visit Eddie.

I'm a publisher. It's what passionately touches my heart. I use words to go forth into the world. It's as much about what I feel in my heart as it is about me carrying the message from the past forward. Now, what you get from that message — what future generations get — that's open. My job is to be a conduit, you see.

By 1978, when Black Classic Press was founded, I had gone through a period of intense reading that made me sure I would focus on Black history. During my reading, I became aware of a lot of books that had gone out of print, and those I felt compelled to bring back into print. My experience in the bookstore helped, when people wanted out-of-print materials. I had a whole catalog in my head of books that were not obtainable at that time.

I still had the bookstore, but it was in pitiful shape. I had started going to Sojourner-Douglass College in 1975. In '78 I just stopped selling books and began to publish pamphlets as Black Classic Press. That's how it started.

Who was I working with when I started Black Classic Press? [*Long pause*] Guilty.

Me. [*Laughs*] It was me. The only other person was my future wife, Cheryl Waters. She always distinguished herself from the press, but she would help me. Basically, though, it was just me.

I wanted to build a list, so I decided to do three pamphlets. I probably didn't start putting them inside book covers until I had about five pamphlets. I wouldn't have had a catalog at that time, just that list. You got to understand that the pamphlets were the books. I'm emphasizing that because it's very consistent with our struggle. When our elders produced what we now call pamphlets, they called them books.

It was as hard getting those things out as it was any book I've ever published. They were saddle-stitched and I would print them in my basement. My kids talk about that now because I would have them help me organize and stitch those books together.

The first real book we did was a hundred-page, perfect-bound book. Wait, it wasn't even perfect bound. It was stapled, saddle-stitched. It was a book called *Survey Graphic: Harlem, Mecca of the New Negro.* I wanted to make sure we published that piece before I went away to library school.

It was first published in 1925 as a magazine, and I published it close to that format.

Survey Graphic was the monthly house journal of a social work organization called Survey Associates that focused on sociology and social work. In 1924, Alain Locke was selected to edit a special edition of the group's journal that focused on the *New Negro* and what was happening, particularly in Harlem, but also around the country.

Alain Locke taking this on at the time was a major thing. The first edition sold about forty thousand copies, which was tremendous for that time. They had to reprint about three times. It ended up being their most popular issue. It formed the basis of the book that Alain Locke would later write, *The New Negro,* which you may be more familiar with. *Survey Graphic* was the first book after the pamphlets that we published, and we still keep it in print.

I Can Write!

EDDIE: This is a story I'm always going to promote, right? I'm inside prison and Ta-Nehisi comes to interview me. He was going to Howard at the time. I think he was in his third year. Paul sent him down to do an article on my case.

See, Paul had already shared with me that Ta-Nehisi was thinking of dropping out of school. So I was supposed to talk to him and encourage him not to.

Like offer an example, "Look what happened to me." [*Eddie and Paul laugh*]

So he came for the interview and we did have that talk. Ta-Nehisi went away and wrote an article. And the article met with such acclaim that he said, "I can write!"

So Ta-Nehisi started writing — *and dropped out of school.* [*Eddie and Paul crack up*]

PAUL: He wasn't much in school, anyway. He was always a boy that would take all these classes but would never, never do the finals. He would go to the classes he liked — and he would be all up inside the classes — but he wasn't taking no final.

EDDIE: You know what he told me? He said, everything he learned, he learned up in your library, Paul. There was like thousands of books in the house where he learned. In fact, he referred to it as being in prison. Because, he said, there was no television. [*Paul explodes, laughing*] "My father kept me up in this room. And I didn't have anything to do but to read."

That Partner Thing

EDDIE: Dominque Stevenson isn't a lot of my public story. She works for the Baltimore American Friends Service Committee [AFSC]. We worked together for years, but I'm careful, because she doesn't want to be seen as an adjunct to me. She wants to be her own person. She's doing her work and always has been.

My first contact with the AFSC was back in '76 or '77, when we taught conflict resolution and the Quakers came in to help us do that. But I didn't know Dominque until 2001.

See, in 2001, Dominque went to a conference in South Africa for the AFSC, around the issues of international race and racism and reparations. In Durban, Dominque came in contact with people from Boston who were campaigning about my case. Then she got in contact with me, and visited me in prison. That was when I first met Dominque. We decided that we could work together to help the prison population.

Then 9/11 happened, and the issue was boots on the ground. We were trying to see if we could stop that war. So Dominque and I created the mentoring program, Friend of a Friend.

I'm not sure just where the idea of a mentoring program came from. First, it was this program against the Iraq War. When we started, we took over a veterans' organization and made it the first antiwar veterans' organization inside the prison system. Around 2002 or 2003, we worked to get the vets in the prison to start mentoring young people.

We figured, who has a more authentic voice than army veterans — especially veterans in jail? All the old vets had skills and knowledge, but they were partying and not giving anything to the prison population. So we asked them, "You went to one Iraq war, you come back home, and now you're in jail. How do you feel?"

They were feeling like nobody else needs to go over there again to another war, that's how.

We also trained people from different street organizations, like the Bloods, Crips, Dead Man Incorporated, to mentor young people. Almost all of them were Black, so we also taught them about their history, about their culture, about the struggle. And we trained them about coming out and giving back to the community.

Friend of a Friend is now in a few state prisons, a couple of federal prisons. Some of the Friend-of-a-Friend people who are out now are with us in Baltimore at Gilmor Homes, doing work in the community. That has an impact on people there that remember them, when they were destroying the community. They have a certain amount of street cred, you know.

When Dominque and I started working together, we also started a long-term relationship. I would describe Dominque as my partner, my life mate, my significant other. She don't like that partner thing, but that's what she is.

I Never Got the *Star Trek* Books

PAUL: I just came across a postcard I brought back from Egypt years ago. It was a beautiful picture of an art thing, and I had written on this postcard something like, "I wanted you to see this in living color." I was going to send it to Eddie — but I didn't. I remember wanting to share that trip with him, but feeling like Eddie couldn't be out to see it.

EDDIE: I don't know. With the kind of time we had, I was probably more focused on, "We need fifteen books — we need this — we need that."

PAUL: But Eddie would always ask me

about my trips and what I was doing. You can't say, "Oh man, I had a tremendous time," you know? Like, I wouldn't tell Eddie that I had a good crab cake. "Oh god, you should have tasted the food, man. It was incredible." Or, "I had great sex and I got this beautiful woman," you know? [*Laughs*] I mean what is the point?

There was always the thought of Eddie getting out, but it wasn't a sure thing. We had to keep moving toward it, but it didn't get real until right before you actually got out.

EDDIE: Yeah, I was close a couple of times, but then the chance evaporated. Like in '93, we actually thought we had a sentence reduction possibility with one judge. Then the judge died on the tennis court —

PAUL: I remember now. We also got close to work release at one point. Very close.

EDDIE: And they shut down the whole program.

PAUL: This would also have been in the '90s. Eddie was up for work release.

EDDIE: I can't remember all the close calls

I went through, but I can remember those two.

PAUL: Work release would only have been one step toward getting out, because Eddie could have been in work release forever.

EDDIE: But I honestly think I went into prison with the idea that I was getting out. I was going to survive this ordeal, no matter what. So many times I actually thought that we were at that door.

That one time, because of all the flaws in the case, it looked like, "OK, I can be resentenced to X amount of years." That would have put me in a position to then go in front of a parole board and maybe get to the work-release program. And the judge died.

PAUL: That was the judge before the one who turned you down.

EDDIE: Yeah. The last denial was after the Unger decision in 2012. I was supposed to get out about a year before. But *Fox News* and the local media ran stories about me being guilty. That made the state snatch my release back. Right?

PAUL: All the way up until the actual walking out the door, there was never any certainty.

EDDIE: Like, if it snows the day of court, the hearing's going to be postponed four more months, and then something else can happen. It was always iffy. I'm sure that contributed to my high blood pressure and stress level. When I got out I weighed like 240 pounds. Probably 60 was just eating-pounds.

I thought I was eating healthy but I was really eating wrong for years. I'm buying stuff out of the commissary: tuna fish, sardines, Ritz crackers, Tasty Cake pies, chicken noodle soup. Somebody might steal a block of cheese; I'd put that in my little cooler. So I'm thinking I'm eating all the right things, but I don't realize that everything is full of sodium. Peanut butter and jelly sandwiches all during the '90s — my blood pressure just went off the chart. Especially when another court case fell through. That was after '93 probably, right Paul?

PAUL: '95?

EDDIE: Something like that. If it hadn't

190

been for Paul, I wouldn't have had anybody to cry on, because I can't cry with people inside the prison. I don't know how it is in women's jails, but in the men's, you can't do that. You can't get a hug. You can beef about stuff but you can't talk about the pain or the loss.

PAUL: To be honest, Eddie never really cried. Never, never cried. I marveled at that because I would have been boo-hooing.

Back in the day — I seem to remember having five kids to take care of and no visible means of contributing to their support. I was so worried. I used to cry to Eddie, "How am I going to make my $41-a-week rent? Cheryl and Ta-Nehisi and me will be out on the street." So I went to Eddie and told him I couldn't be out organizing, and that he'd have to be responsible. He immediately took that on. I also knew that I just was not going to be the one outside carrying signs, and messing with all them crazy people.

EDDIE: Don't go that way. [*Chuckling*]

PAUL: I wanted to be clear that I was not leaving him, you know. I'll always be your support and be there for you, but I knew I couldn't mess with those people and do chicken dinners and stuff. Not anymore. There had to be a better way.

EDDIE: I was also doing community activism at the time I was working on my own case. From the time I stepped in the door I was engaged with both the inside and the outside community, and that kept me sane and strengthened. Like, in '77, I remember people went to the United Nations about political prisoners and had a big campaign. Not that we thought anything would come of it.

PAUL: I think Dominque should also be recognized as a sustaining force in Eddie's life. You can imagine being locked down and having ideas and not being able to get them into action. She's given many of his ideas life. In fact, Dominque is a large reason Eddie's here with us now.

EDDIE: Yeah, when people want to know the Panther history, the prison struggle, I recognize her work and how we work together. But I try to leave her with her individuality.

PAUL: With Dominque, Eddie had someone

he could trust to do what she said she was going to do. After all those years, Dominque cleared the deck.

EDDIE: See, years ago I had been trying to write a book. I had decided, "Damn, I could die here, and all of my life is going to be lost." So I wrote everything down. I sent my writing to Paul, and a month later I asked him about it.

He said, "Brother, I tried to read it five times and it put me to sleep." It was that bad. I sent it to another friend and supporter, Tom Cullota, a white community organizer at the community center, and he fell asleep on it. I sent it to about five people and it put everybody to sleep. So I put that book away. A while later, I thought, "You know, maybe I can tackle this first book again." So I pulled it out — and *I* went to sleep.

Then, about thirty-three years into my sentence — there was a point I was so low. I don't talk about this a lot, but that was probably the only time I lost hope I would ever get out. At that point, I had at least three support committees, and they were all fighting each other about who was in charge, and what we should do, and it was driving me insane.

PAUL: That was probably the only time you expressed anger and didn't feel that people were handling the case well.

EDDIE: By then, I had met Dominque. I remember it exactly. I said to Dominque, "Fuck this. I'm not struggling with all these crazy-ass people. I'm just going to read! Go buy me one thousand *Star Trek* books. I'll be OK. I'm gonna line them up in my cell and just read until I'm ninety. I'll know everything about *Star Trek*. I will be the expert and then I'll die."

I had a support network that would have provided that. I also told Dominque, "By the way, I got a book here but it's so bad it put every one of the people who love me to sleep."

She said, "Let me look at it." And she breathed life into my writing. She twinked it and she got all in my business, and we got it published.

Right then, I realized that Dominque was the one. Because she was so brilliant. This might be a male chauvinist thing — I was always surprised and impressed with the amount she knew. I'm like, "Damn, you know everything."

Earlier, I fell in love with her mind, but not her. I would spend hours on the phone

194

talking to her and she would push back. But the book was when I realized, "This is somebody I can count on." We started having a serious relationship then.

But I never got the *Star Trek* books.

■ ■ ■ ■

Part III

■ ■ ■ ■

There are years that ask questions and
years that answer.
— Zora Neale Hurston,
Their Eyes Were Watching God

Part III

CHAPTER 11:
PAUL AND EDDIE
AND THEN THE WORLD

Year upon year, Eddie, with Paul and assorted lawyers and support committees, devised political and legal campaigns aimed at winning Eddie his freedom. Nothing worked. In 1975 Paul started college and by 1980 had earned a Masters in Library Science. That same year, Jackie Powell, Eddie's codefendant, died inside prison, of heart failure.[1] Eddie continued organizing and mentoring.

More years passed and Eddie's son, Ronald, became the father of two boys. His second son, Deshawn, made Eddie a grandfather again with the birth of twin girls. Paul's partner, Cheryl Waters, gave Ta-Nehisi a baby brother, Menelik, the seventh of Paul's children. As Paul started work at Howard University's Moorland-Spingarn Research Center,[2] Black Classic Press began taking off, publishing poignant, hard-to-find history by writers such as Yosef Ben-Jochannan and David Walker, as well as original work by the likes of Bobby

Seale and Walter Mosley.

Two of Eddie's nephews were in and out of prison. Eddie's mother died and he wasn't allowed to attend her funeral.

In 2010 Jack Johnson, having been resentenced, maxed out his time and left prison. Paul Coates remembers picking Jack up when he got out and putting him on a plane to Chicago, so he could be with his mother before she died.

Eddie kept working. He earned three college degrees. He waited for those *Star Trek* books . . .

Then in May 2012, the Maryland Court of Appeals issued a ruling in *Unger v. State of Maryland.* Prisoners could have their cases reviewed if they had been convicted before 1980 in felony trials where judges had told juries that they need not consider guidelines such as "beyond a reasonable doubt" in rendering a verdict. People who had lived most of their lives behind bars could now appeal to have their convictions overturned. Gradually, a few — their average age was 64 — started to get out.

Adjectives like "landmark," "watershed," and "game-changer" have been applied to the Unger decision, which continues to give Maryland prisoners — most now geriatric lifers — the hope of release. At the time I'm writing this, the Unger decision has allowed 193 people serving life sentences in Maryland to walk free. So far, only one has committed a new crime.[3]

Unger was hardly the long-awaited exoneration that Eddie Conway might have dreamed of. It offered a legal technicality as faint promise of a life outside, with justice a possible afterthought. But Unger may have been his last best chance of getting out. Eddie recalls:

> We had been fighting our case for years, and every time we won, the state fought back. So we said, "OK, we won Unger. How do we unravel this?"

As the state of Maryland began a rotation of hearings based on individual cases, Robert Boyle and Phillip G. Dantes, Eddie's lawyers at the time, filed a motion in light of the Unger decision, arguing for Eddie's release. Eddie and Paul, meanwhile, wondered how or if Eddie's case would fit into the mix:

> EDDIE: At first, Maryland said they were going to release seven people each month, so the state could absorb the transitions. My case was supposed to be heard in June, but Fox ran those cop-

killer news stories about me on television, and the state snatched my case out of the rotation. They said my case was so high profile, it would damage the rest of the guys getting out. It was Bob Boyle that forced them to put me back in the rotation.

PAUL: They kept stringing you along. We were certain you'd be out by Thanksgiving. It just didn't work. And once they pulled the case back, you became uncertain.

Finally, about nine months later, Eddie was granted a hearing. He was to be brought to court, before a judge.

PAUL: But it wasn't a guaranteed release.

EDDIE: None of them is ever a guaranteed release. Every time we went up there all those years, it was uncertain.

In a conceivably cosmic sign that his life might have come full circle, Eddie's hearing took place at 111 N. Calvert Street — the old downtown Baltimore Post Office where Eddie was working the night of his arrest. It had since been revamped into a circuit courthouse and now, on March 4, 2014, here Eddie was again.

I remember the day as being clear and cold, with clumps of grayish snow lining Baltimore's sidewalks. Laura and I were there early. The courtroom had the worn, municipal feel of an old-timey schoolroom, downgraded for legal purposes.

Not too many people, maybe forty, were there, because this hearing had to be kept under the radar. The prospect of a notorious "Panther cop-killer" being released from prison doesn't happen often. If word spread too far, there could be media vigilantes and vengeful police supporters showing up, absolutely convinced that someone like Eddie Conway should die in prison. Eddie's son, Ronald, had come. There were some of his longtime friends, a few community activists — some whose young lives Eddie had transformed when they were in prison with him. Dominque was there, of course. And sitting one row behind us was Paul Coates.

Judge Barry Williams entered, having already presided over a number of Unger hearings. Then Eddie was brought in and hustled to the defense table. We could only see his back. Boyle and Dantes approached the bench and began talking quietly to the judge.

For maybe forty minutes, Laura and I strained to hear and comprehend the legal palaver up-front. I was just about to give up when, ever so quietly, it happened. The judge said Eddie could go.

I saw Eddie maybe ten minutes later, on the sidewalk outside, surrounded by a mini-mob of friends, comrades, lawyers, and well-wishers. He was wearing a handsome leather jacket. And he was hugging Paul.

They Pushed Me Out

EDDIE: The courtroom was a blur, but I knew a lot of my friends was there. Because when you go in, you got leg irons on, you got handcuffs on, there's guards on both sides of you. You come out of a quiet hallway into a bright-lighted room with, it seemed like, hundreds of people. You don't get to actually see that much, except maybe a few people on the first three rows or something.

I had some hope but I also had a dread that something would derail this. Because we had been up this mountain fifteen, twenty times, and each time we got near the summit, there was a landslide of some sort, and we'd end up back down in the valley. I knew my release was supposed to happen — but it was supposed to happen multiple times before.

I was scheduled to go to court that morning at ten o'clock but I was kept sitting in that bullpen and they never called me upstairs. I was probably like four hours late — that was part of being apprehensive. Probably around two o'clock, they called me.

Then it was like, "Hey, you. Get up." "Let's go, we got to go!" "Don't worry; you'll be OK."

I can't honestly say that I focused on anybody in particular. You try to acknowledge people, but it's a crowd. You see a blur of faces and then you're up at the front and you're sitting down with your back to everybody.

It happened too fast to evaluate. The judge did the gavel thing and said I could go. They got me up from the chair. I went out the courtroom. They said, "Not the front door" — they let me out a side door. Then down the hall, on the elevator. They took me downstairs to the basement, up to a desk. They said, "Give me that shirt. Give me this. You can't have —" They snatched off my sweatshirt, they took my prison jacket.

Then it was, "See that door over there? Go out that door." They pushed me out. I didn't have any ID or anything. It happened so fast, it was *zoom!* I come out the door and luckily there was people out there. Dominque was there at the door when I came out.

That jacket I had on outside? One of the guys on the sidewalk took off his jacket and gave it to me. Wahid, from Friend of a Friend — he was one of the comrades that was in jail with me. Because when I came out that door, I had on just a pair of jeans and a t-shirt. That's what the deal was.

I didn't get to see hardly anybody, maybe a dozen people or so. Paul, Dantes, Boyle. And then they hustled me away. I went up the street and around the corner, and I was gone. I'm probably still in disbelief, because my feet never touched the ground, so to speak. I think everybody wanted to get me away from the courthouse.

I hadn't been exposed to stuff outside. I'm still apprehensive about how I'm going to cope with all this — what it's all going to mean and what's new for me? At the party that night I was still feeling my way around. I was just meeting people and it was still all a blur because it was so many different stimuli. I remember Paul showing me how his cell phone worked.

The first person I talked to on that phone was Walter Mosley. Paul had told him about me and he had supported my case for years. Paul said, "Here, talk to Walter."

I Didn't Trust the Process

PAUL: My job was to keep things quiet. The deal was to restrict people from coming, not let them know that Eddie was actually gonna have that hearing. We were concerned that people would come in and disrupt things. And the cops were definitely a concern. The fact that they didn't show up en masse is kind of unbelievable.

There were so many people who would have wanted to know that Eddie was getting out. People who had stood with us for years. And I couldn't tell them — I couldn't even swear people to secrecy because they might slip and tell somebody. The most I could say is that we probably are going to have a very big announcement in a few days. So that was trying. I felt I was betraying the people who deserved to be in that courtroom. But it was a necessary kind of betrayal.

As it turned out, I was very surprised to walk in the court and see people there.

Actually, I believed that there would be another denial. I didn't believe we'd come this far and that Eddie's release was actually gonna happen. I only half believed he would ever walk out. That feeling of half-belief stayed with me, I would say, for months.

I can't remember the words the judge spoke when he released him — but when Eddie was released and they said they were going to take him downstairs? I didn't think he was going to be there. I didn't trust the process.

There was no reason for me to trust. Every time before, when we thought Eddie was going to get out — no matter how close we thought we were — it didn't work. I mean, when he thought he was going to get out in 2012, that was after a process that had gone on probably two years before that. I didn't trust this time, either, even though I heard what they said. In my brain they were going to come up with something else. Something they had been holding. I don't think that's so farfetched.

It was real to hug him. It was real for him to be out, but it didn't feel permanent. It felt like it was going to be disrupted, you know? It was this political disbelief.

Because I wasn't prepared for him to get out. [*Laughs*] I was more prepared to keep on visiting him in jail. But he was out in spite of my disbelief. The fact of the matter was he was out and it was real. You know, it's like being in love. You got this amazing woman and she loves you. And you keep saying, "How could she *love* me?"

Not Just Any Place

The judge said Eddie could go.

Go — where?

Too often, home for someone coming out of prison is effectively nowhere. Laws can prevent formerly incarcerated people from living in public housing, even if their families already live there; landlords can refuse to rent to anyone with a record. There's often simply no room among family, or a family has ceased to exist.

But Paul Coates had seen to it that Eddie had a place to live. And not just any place.

In 1984, Paul and Cheryl bought a house in Baltimore, on Tioga Parkway. They lived there with their children for about eight years. When they moved, they still owned the house. Years after, even when he could have sold it for some much-needed cash, Paul held on to this house, thinking that someday, Eddie would need a place to live in and call home.

It was because of Paul — the guy who'd once been thrown out on the street with his family — that Eddie went home.

Ok, What Do We Do Today?

EDDIE: Back at the house on Tioga Parkway, the news people were around the house for the first couple of days. But we kind of ignored them, because it was Fox and they were definitely not trying to do a positive story. So we started getting the house adjusted because it had been mothballed for like six years. Wahid and the rest of the brothers and Dominque went in there and helped dust it off and make it presentable. After my first day or so, I was surprised because I just felt normal. I felt like, "OK, what do we do today?"

Paul took me by the hand and chaperoned me through the first couple of weeks. He said, "You need shoes. You need pants. You need a comb to comb your hair." He showed me where you can get the best Chinese food, where you can get pastries. We went out and bought stuff for the house, like a microwave oven, because there were so many things I needed. For the first few weeks, we spent a lot of time together getting me acclimated.

Dominque was there the whole time. We were in a relationship, so the first thing I did was spend some time with her. At that time, the Fraternal Order of Police had put out a kind of unofficial hit on me, saying that I shouldn't be allowed to walk the streets of Baltimore. It was code for "Get rid of him as soon as you can."

So Dominque organized some bodyguards for me who we knew from Friend of a Friend, and they went with me when I went places. She was my partner in helping me. Paul was kind of the supervisor, but she was the person there on the ground.

Bed in That Good Space

EDDIE: When they kicked me out the prison door, I had no ID, no medicine. But there was this network of people that said, "Come, what do you need? I'm a doctor, I'll write you a prescription. What ID you need? We'll take you to the DMV."

PAUL: Well, I think there's something about Eddie — a charisma — I'm going to use that word. From the time he went to jail, folks shined on him. I think it's because of his charisma people loved him. They really, really loved him.

EDDIE: Honestly, a little pushback on that? I was always concerned about doing the work. I was never only, "Help. Get me out."

PAUL: But people were able to detect something and you did not disappoint. You were principled; you were self-sacrificing. Probably some other stuff in there.

EDDIE: My birthday is over —

PAUL: Still, it's that charisma, man. I mean — you still got it.

EDDIE: But when I came home, what helped me more than anything is that there was a house there. I didn't have to worry about where home was, so it took only a couple of days to adjust. That first day, I never went to sleep at all. The second day, I fell asleep and I slept in my bed. In the middle of the night I woke up and realized — I'm good. I'm all right now. Most of that, I owe to Paul.

I can remember when Paul was struggling to keep that house.

PAUL: Cheryl and I bought that house in 1984. Then we moved to another place. Yeah, at different times, I was broke. I was saying, *Damn.*

EDDIE: And he had a business. This house on Tioga Parkway was just setting there, empty. I said to him several times, "Paul, rent that house out. If it's making you money, it's an asset. Put some old people in there and they won't mess it up." This is when I thought I was young, apparently.

But he just refused to put anybody in there. I felt bad because I know it was draining. And I never knew when I was going to get out. But it is that very house that gave me the stability I need to be here. That bed in that space, that good space. To be in, to relax, to feel secure. From day one, when I got out of prison and got that key, it's been my house.

PAUL: The real deal was, at different times I did have people live in that house. I even lived there after Cheryl and I separated in 2001. But that whole time he was in prison I knew, if he was going to be released, he would need a place to call his home, a place he could come home to. It was important for me that Eddie could always know that he had a home. No matter who came or went, he always knew that. For me to give that house up was not thinkable, because it would have taken a cog out of the whole plan.

When Cheryl and I separated, I moved back in. Then I had to figure out, "After Eddie gets released, can I live in this house with this guy?" [*Laughter*]

Fortunately, my present wife saved me. I moved to DC to be with her, and *he* got to have the whole house. [*More laughter*]

A New Person out of Pookie

EDDIE: So I got out, and the world I saw was shocking. Instead of advancing forty years, the world had deteriorated forty years. Driving through Baltimore and looking at the houses and the people was devastating to me. It looked like a war zone.

Pennsylvania Avenue was always the ghetto and it looked bad, but North Avenue, which is the main street in Baltimore, running from east to west, was horrifying. Block after block after block was destroyed. Up around Johns Hopkins Hospital, going east toward Bellaire, all that was devastated. Houses were falling in, there was no roofs. Trees growing out of some of the houses.

When I was little, I lived around there. It was always the Black community, but there was businesses, there was shops. It was an economic zone that was operational and full of people, full of merchandise. When I got locked up, this was the neighborhood you moved to if you had a good job and some financial security. And it had just collapsed.

Even though a good segment of the Black

population had moved into the middle class, the community was in shambles. The housing stock, the poverty level, the drug epidemic — these things just shocked me. It changed my perspective of what I would do. That's probably why I landed at *The Real News,* working as a reporter.

I can remember Paul advising me — he's been advising me for forty years, even though I'm his elder — "Don't let the world control your narrative and use that 'cop-killer' thing. Change that narrative to looking forward, not back." So now, I'm looking forward to: How am I going to save this thirteen-year-old, that twelve-year-old? How can I try to mend this community so that people have a chance?

Now that I'm out of prison, I see how power works out here, less directly and less visibly. But also, when I was in prison, I counseled so many people, and I saw a light come on in their eyes. They would say, "Damn. If somebody had talked to me like this two years ago, I wouldn't be locked up here." That resonated with me.

I know this is bad to say, but I've spent a lot of time tweaking grown people, and I've realized that often their damage is beyond repair. Even when you can kind of fix it, if you can't invest all your time and be inside a person's problems, it'll still go awry. So I'm into this idea that it's better to build strong young people than to fix broken older people. It's not on the cheap, but it's more likely to be successful.

This is a case of a whole generation of parents disappeared, into the crack hole or the AIDS hole or the prison system or upward mobility. People went in all those four ways. You can't fault people. If you could get out of Section 8 and put your children in a better environment, why wouldn't you? Or if you didn't, what's wrong with you? But then that leaves the school-to-prison pipeline. So I know that the secret is catching them before they get caught up in the system.

Comparing kids I worked with inside prison in the '80s who were so demoralized, to the kids I see outside now, I see better and worse. Whereas in the '80s I just saw me-me-me, get my money, screw everybody — that Ronald Reagan thing — now I see that there's a lot of young people starting to see what's wrong, and how they don't fit into society, and what they can do to change it. I see a new consciousness, a commitment to make a different future. But today, it's more, "I want to be comfortable; I need to get my degree. So I'm not dropping out;

I'm buying in. But I still want to make things better." That's a new breed.

We, in our time, wanted to change the world, but we didn't want to be comfortable in the process. Today, even kids who can't get in, want in. They don't want to be hustling, dealing drugs, but they don't see other options.

Let's say you see some hypothetical kid who's in trouble on the street. Let's call him Pookie. Yeah, Pookie.

Pookie's always in trouble. You see something in this person that you actually like, but Pookie is a mess. How do you handle it?

What I do is try to focus on changing narratives of young people. If they're growing up in a hostile environment — traumatic-stress communities like Gilmor Homes, for instance — then I try to make that environment better, try to let them see different role models.

The Black Lives Matter people, they are not the kids in trouble, in most cases. They're the ones that's community activists or in college. They live in middle-class households, or they grew up in suburbia, the children of professional classes. They've been protected to some degree, or they've scrambled and made their way to a professional level. They're different than Pookie and his crew. And they don't mix.

I've sometimes said that we don't have restorative justice models in Pookie's community. Those models work more in suburbia or wealthier areas: "OK, you broke my window. Here, wash the car this week." You break a window in Pookie's community, you go to jail for two years. Or you end up in juvie somewhere. Young people in Pookie's circles have a fatalism. Black Lives Matter people tend not to. So what I've been doing is taking Black Lives Matter people down to Pookie. And I'm actually impressed with them.

This Thanksgiving, we gave away over a hundred turkeys and bags of food, and the Black Lives Matter folks were right down there, giving out the turkeys. Now, it's not even near Christmas, and they've already collected up a hundred and twenty-five coats.

I also teach the Black Lives Matter people in classes out at Coppin [State University] and over at Morgan [State University], about theory versus practice. I say, "You can't always point out what's wrong. You can't have policy ideas and debating skills if you don't do anything."

They're actually changing. They're young,

they're Black, they're energetic, and they're starting to be OK. They're talking about leadership, consciousness, about police violence. They're also talking about the need to be in the community and doing stuff with Pookie. That's what I tell them: "If you don't go and help Pookie, Pookie gonna come and help you." [*Laughs*]

I'm not seeing a big Black Lives Matter impact on Pookie's community yet. It's too early. Bernie Sanders was just down at Gilmor Homes, with an entourage of about a hundred people. In front of Freddie Gray's mural, where Bernie went for his photo op, there was this little band of about seven Black Lives people, protesting.

"We need jobs. When you going to give us decent housing?" — the spiel we were saying in the '60s. They had their signs up. Really baby steps. Seven people out there, and we're looking at a community that's thousands of people. It's a slow process, but I'm beginning to see Pookie getting politicized a little. Even Pookie Senior.

There's a guy at Gilmor — Pookie Senior — that lost his mother, and we went to see him down there today. Many, many people came from far and near to greet the brother, people from all over the neighborhood. "Our condolences," and such. Us guys was there on the corner talking with Pookie Senior. We were telling him and his friends, "We're gonna put a Christmas tree up down here for the children. What you think?"

One of the elders say, "Uhh, don't bring no tree down here because they'll steal it."

Then we tell the younger guys about the tree and they say, "Yeah, put it up on December 20th. It'll be OK. Let the kids decorate it. We got you." They put the word out: Don't mess with that tree.

That's because Pookie's starting to recognize the need to be concerned about the community, about the young children.

Honestly, everybody thinks, "These old political organizers are trying to make the young people follow in their footsteps." No, these young people want to get out, themselves. They don't want to be in this environment, but they don't have a way out. I don't see them becoming highly politicized, but I do see them becoming conscious about their community and the need to work together.

A year before I got out, Dominque had ex-prisoners down there at Gilmor, doing a free lunch program. These guys were giving out sandwiches and bag lunches to people. After I got out, I went there and noticed that, years before, these same guys handing

out the lunches had terrorized the neighborhood. Everybody knew who they were —
"Oh man, that's Bootie Green. He's bad."

But the people in the neighborhood see
him now giving out sandwiches. It's like,
"OK, this is a new person here."

Who Got a Problem with the Court?

EDDIE: After I started to work with these
kids, we organizers said to each other, "We
need to stabilize and center this." So we
picked a busted basketball court, where we
were giving out food, as a sort of base to
operate from.

Actually, people had been trying to get
that court fixed for like eighteen years: "Be
nice if we had this basketball court fixed up.
A basketball court would give the young
people something to do."

So I said, "No biggie. You want the court
fixed? Let's get a work order . . ."

For about a year, nothing happened.
Everybody — our city councilman, the city
council president — they ran us all over the
place. Finally, we got so frustrated we
decided to go in there and dig up the court
— in violation of the city ordinance — just
dig the whole damn thing up and put a new
court in there. We had a lawyer with us, and
the young guys there were saying to the city,

"You all better not come down here and be messin' with us."

So we put a new court in. Of course, as soon as it's in, the city says: "We're going to meet and decide what we're going to do about this basketball court."

Eighteen years. And now suddenly you done found the will to make a decision? The chief housing officials were saying, "We're going to decide whether we want to remove this. We don't want the liability. We don't want the workers to get hurt. We need to look at the budget. We need a board of estimate meeting. And somebody needs to insure it."

We said, "We been asking you to look at it and you ain't seen it yet. *We'll* insure it."

So these officials called everybody to this big meeting, and all the young guys went. I had to tell them to chill out — cause when those young guys rolled up in there, they were saying: "*Who* got a problem with the court?"

I kept telling them, *"Don't scare the people."*

But the young guys say, "You all mess with this court, there's going to be some gunfire down here."

And the city said, "Actually, we think you all should keep it." [*Laughs*]

So it may not be quite legal, but it's a done deal. Ain't nobody going to mess with it. It's *there,* you know? There's people who want to be there all the time, and they're loving it. Nobody in the neighborhood had a problem with it.

Except, of course, the police. They didn't want it because they said the basketball court would attract drug activities. Which is the dumbest thing in the world. For the last eighteen years, all around the basketball court, there's drug activity. I can go down there and throw a rock and hit somebody selling drugs. So what kind of sense does saying you can't have a basketball court make? But police say, "Some young kid will get hurt down there."

I'm saying they can get hurt down there anyway, just walking through.

In My Male Stuff

PAUL: In his first book, Ta-Nehisi wrote about me, when I was in the Panthers, telling my quote-unquote "legal" wife, Linda, just after she had just given birth to my first son, that another woman in the Panther Party was also pregnant with my child. I told Linda this, when she had just delivered my son, because I didn't want to do it while she was pregnant. But I was busting to be open with this. Ta-Nehisi said my timing may have been a little off. He's right. But I carried the damn stuff as long as I could.

It's really, really, tough, translating where my mindset was, and fitting it into an explanation today, without losing the context. What were we thinking?

I don't have the full answer. I'm going to have to go back to the women and get their stories. I can't talk about how difficult it was; what it meant to them; why they participated in — whatever.

For my part, I'm clear that, one, I was prepared to be in multiple relationships. I came up with a father who was in multiple relationships; wasn't anything wrong in my mind with that. Two, I came up at a time when this whole country — many, many young people — were enrolled in the notion of overturning a society that, on one hand, oppressed Black people and, on the other hand, could be monstrous enough to create the Vietnam War. A lot of our looking for the source of this was rooted in a socialist analysis that had to do with the rejection of the state. That meant rejecting the notion of ownership — of men owning women; women owning men. There was that "smash monogamy" stuff. That's why, across the country, we had communes. It wasn't anything for people to have multiple relationships because it was their choice. Choice was the thing. Inside the Party, there wasn't any ownership of women. Theoretically.

There was a term for it in the Party. "Who are you relating to?"

"Are you relating to anybody, sister?"

The first sister I related to would have been Patsy. It wasn't inside of commitment. I was married to Linda at the time, but that was outside the Party. Inside the Party, my relationship with Patsy was primary, but even that had its limits, because she could have related to who she wanted to. It wasn't a thing she had to tell me. I did not own her or her body.

In the Party, everyone knew that. Nobody was hiding that stuff. So I was straddled between the commitment I had as a husband and the relationship I had in the Party. It wasn't like I'd been a church mouse. Still, the timing was not great.

I know all that happened in a context where men have more power than women. I can't answer to that; this is part of my confusion. I can't answer because I'm still in my male stuff. I see this as a man, and I'm not looking at the power differential.

But I don't want to totally lose the male stuff, because that's dishonest, too.

The Fact That I Fucked up Her Life . . .

PAUL: Back in the day, I sometimes thought of Linda as being — you know how we'd say — Black bourgeois. She wasn't, of course. If anything, she was Black middle-working or lower-working class with aspirations. And back then we called anyone Black that had anything or aspired to anything middle-class, bourgeois.

When we first married, I had aspirations, too. I traded them in when I went into the Panthers. When I came back to Baltimore after the Panthers, after Oakland, we were living in the projects. I'd been expelled from the Panther Party and I didn't know what I was going to do. I had three children with Linda and two children outside of our marriage. Eddie and the others were in jail. My politics were scrambled. I had no money, no job, and not a lot of hope. I was in a haze, not knowing what to do. Linda helped clear up the haze. She got rid of me.

We used to argue quite a bit, but *I* thought, even still, we were actually having a great time. One day, she sent me up the hill to her mother's house to get something, I don't know what. Her mother lived a few blocks from the projects in her own house, in Westport.

I went up there. I loved her mother; her

226

mother loved me. So we talked about stuff and I went back down the hill.

I went to open the door; the door wouldn't open.

I knock on the door quietly several times, because I don't want people to hear me banging trying to get in. But Linda didn't open the door, so I get a little bit louder. She still didn't come. I say, "What's up with this?"

I walk back up to her mother's house to call her. I say, "Linda, you're not opening the door." She said, "Right, I'm not opening the door."

I say, "Well, Linda, I'm going to come back down there and would you please open the door?"

Her mother gets on the phone and talks to her and says, "Coates, she'll open the door."

I go back down the hill and she still won't open the door. At this point, I'm banging on the door, and I don't care who hears me. "Linda, Linda, let me in the house!"

"I'm not letting you in the house!"

"Let me in the house — what is wrong with you?"

"I'm not letting you in the house. Why don't you go on down to Pennsylvania Avenue?"

At that point we had set up the George Jackson Prison Movement office on Pennsylvania Avenue. So I decided, I'll go. But I'm pissed, and now I want my clothes, my few items of possession. I say, "I'll go, just open the door and let me get my stuff."

"Your stuff is across the street in the dumpster. [*Laughs*]

I couldn't believe it. I went over and retrieved my stuff. Then I sat down on the steps and I said, "Damn. She's totally crazy." I made my way to the office, set up a place in the back, and I lived in the George Jackson Prison office. The point is, I just thought she was crazy. I really did not understand her actions at the time. It became one of those things I filed away but did not spend a lot of time with.

Until one day I was thinking about it and it all began to make sense. It would have made sense then but I was too far gone in my revolutionary stuff. Thinking now, I said, "Look. She didn't marry me to be in the projects, or for me to end up in the Panther Party, the cops chasing me, and me having children with other women. That's not why she married me."

I had knocked her up with three kids. She's not working; she's on welfare, which I had forced her on by not providing for her or my children. I've got her living in the projects a few blocks from her mother, who's having the life she once had. My actions or inactions, regardless of how I felt about them at the time, had real impact on her life. I had fucked it up. Whatever notion of family and raising children she had was replaced by the hopelessness of living in the projects. And in my haze, I was not showing her anything better — no hope, no change.

At the time, the fact that I had fucked up her life never occurred to me. Why wouldn't she come to a decision to throw me out? Here's the funny part. Years — I mean years — later, I had this revelation, and I'm saying, "Damn, why didn't this occur to me at the time?" I go in and I talk with Linda.

She remembers none of this! [*Paul laughs hugely*]

229

CHAPTER 12:
ARE YOU STILL A
REVOLUTIONARY?

"Are you or are you not a Revolutionary?" This question, or variations of it, has taken up immense blocks of time and thought among radicals of assorted stripes, as they sit down, alone or with each other, to work out: Just what does my commitment to changing the world mean?

Every answer is doomed at some point to be judged as incorrect. But, as it is among most people who follow their own paths, there is a large amount of agreement inside Paul's and Eddie's differences. This conversation took place a few months after a string of arrests linked to protests of police killings of African Americans across the country, including the 2015 murder of Freddie Gray, in Baltimore.

Are You Still a Revolutionary?

PAUL: I don't call myself a revolutionary now. I left that behind many years ago, because my notion of revolution and what I wanted out of life was not the same.

I wanted my family, you know? I wanted to make sure that those I had brought into the world had a life. I was not the person to stand out in front of the jail with a sign, calling for revolution.

Early on in Eddie's incarceration, the impact of having kids caused a paternal thing to kick off. Clearly, I wasn't the one that was going to die for the people. I would die for what I believed in, but what "the people" were and the nature of "the struggle" — ? My experience in the Panther Party showed I didn't know what the hell that was.

I could call myself someone who was conscious, who had political feelings and made commitments around politics. But I certainly didn't know what "revolutionary" was. To be honest, I still don't.

EDDIE: And just the opposite, I'm probably still a revolutionary. But I think I would rather not be.

I still believe in change; I still desire a new world. At the same time, I'm too old to be out anywhere. Also, I can no longer be pigeonholed into this Marxism, that Maoism, this Che-Guevara-ism, or even anarchism. I have a vision for tomorrow, but I know that's a thousand years away.

As far as I'm concerned, healing the neighborhood is revolutionary. If you can help make our neighborhood whole, and make our children safe, that's revolutionary in the middle of a collapsing, drug-induced, AIDS-infected society.

PAUL: I don't disagree. But to make some place safe is not revolutionary to me. I wouldn't call myself a revolutionary based on that.

I know what you're talking about; I'm committed to that as well. I'm committed to something where justice reigns, but I have no idea what that means in reality. So I don't think that makes me a revolutionary. I guess I hold revolution as a process that people are committed to in a 24/7, unending way. They're ready to spend their lives for that, right?

EDDIE: Yeah, and I don't think that's fair. I don't think that's what revolutionaries are. That's the image and the consciousness that we had as Panthers — as youth, as children. That romanticized thing that captured us. But looking back thousands of years, what I see now is that "revolutionary" means different things in different times, in different settings. The guy that broke his slave chain and ran away was a revolutionary. Even if he run all the way to Canada and then went back to get his wife and children. That was revolutionary for that system and that time.

Actually, I think Paul doesn't see the rippling effects of Black Classic Press. Of course, the consciousness comes from other presses and media too, but all that good work is changing our future. It's a long-term thing, but you can see this sea change of attitudes around the world among the young. I think that's revolutionary work.

PAUL: But see what you said: "revolutionary work." I don't disagree with that. The question is, Am I a revolutionary? This is a whole nother thing. Because what I do today, I might give up in the next second. Same thing about the books that Black Classic Press publishes. Of course, anyone with a head and a heart who wants to get something out of them could — but it's not done for white people; it's done for the Black community. If you say that's revolutionary, that's fine. Those actions may be revolutionary. That enslaved African who broke his chains and ran away and then went back to get his wife — you can say he's a revolutionary all you want to. But: "That's my baby, I *love* her." [*Laughter*]

EDDIE: But that man's fighting to change the system. He's saying *this* should be *that*. I know this is corny; it's Che Guevara's thing: "Revolutionaries are guided by true feelings of love for the people." Back in our day, the deal was, nothing else was important. I could overlook people's faults. I was so in love with the people that I didn't really have love for the individual.

PAUL: Was that a mistake?

EDDIE: I don't know that it was a mistake, but it certainly stole something from me. At the time, I think it was probably what motivated all of us, the entire movement, to make change for the future. You were soldiers for The Revolution. But every generation produces that; every generation needs to produce that. We would still be enslaved if there weren't those people saying, "No, we're going to change this, whatever the cost."

PAUL: If you're saying that a real revolutionary is motivated by love, OK. But what is happening now? I'm a bit more concerned about all of the Black Lives Matter people going to jail now and getting charges. Nobody's keeping track of them. Looking forward, what is the structure that's going to be there for them? People are getting busted all over this country. Young activists these days have been getting charges and they've been getting time.

EDDIE: Yeah, terrorism and everything —

PAUL: All kinds of crazy charges. Lots of these young folks have never had a political party, so they don't have an ideology equal to what they're protesting out in the street. These people can get lost. This is the part that's straight up-and-down harder for me.

EDDIE: The other side is state violence, like what the government used to split the Party. State violence like the murder of Fred Hampton. The blowing up of the Panther office in Des Moines. The killing of Tamir Rice and Sandra Bland. That's state violence. State violence is constant and consistent.

Now look at the Black Lives Matter movement. In this one California case, this woman was trying to pull someone back from being arrested after a demonstration, and she got a "felony lynching" charge.[1] That's state violence. Here in Baltimore, a guy took a trashcan and threw it through the window of a cop car during this public reaction to Freddie Gray's murder. He got a half-a-million-dollar bail.[2] I lost track of him, 'cause he fell into the system. He got time —

PAUL: Like a dozen years or something?

EDDIE: Yeah, he's in the system, he's disappeared, and there's no one and nothing outside supporting him. All kinds of people are going to jail around this stuff, like Paul was saying. And there's no network out here to focus on that.

PAUL: I was with a group of Black Lives Matter folks some weeks ago at the Kennedy Center in DC. They were talking about their cases, saying, "Well, so-and-so is representing me; who's representing you?"
I asked them, "Are you guys tracking the people who get arrested?"
They said, "Yeah! We know all the people who got arrested."
I said, "Nationally?"
"No, no. Ferguson."

But I'm asking, "Who's doing this nation-ally?"

EDDIE: There is no national network. There's a movement that's made up of a hundred different groups with a hundred different ideologies, all the way from the Dream Defenders to the Cop Watch thing.

PAUL: To me, it's a question for the future, not the past. The resistance has been crushed and jailed in a way that it wasn't in our time. There was a network back then that knew names, knew incidents. We can talk about Leonard Peltier now because of the consciousness we developed. That's not happening with young folks.

EDDIE: You know what's dangerous about that? That man or woman who steps up in defense of the community and takes some action ends up in the prison system. They're isolated and alone.[3]

PAUL: That's right.

EDDIE: And they become angry with the community for abandoning them. Not only that, but they get ridiculed among the other prisoners: "You're stupid, that's dumb."

That's negative reinforcement for supporting the community. That's dangerous —

PAUL: The other part is the non-acknowledgment of the person. That kills the example for the future. In other words, if you don't acknowledge Leonard Peltier, then there's no legacy for the next person who goes to jail. So the extermination of a person caught up in the prison system is complete. That form of resistance becomes just that much more threatened and the legacy of resistance as future action is at stake.

EDDIE: Other prisoners will say, "You're crazy. Study what? Read what? I don't care about you."

PAUL: Does this generation of Black activists have a respect for, on one hand, the legacy of the Panthers and, on the other hand, the current movements? Yes, absolutely. But it's very decentralized. You end up talking with leaders who are not really leaders. You talk to formations that come together around smoke.

EDDIE: That smoke you see is the stirring of a movement, but it's not a movement yet.

People will hopefully create something with substance, but it has to be built. Right now, we're mostly seeing protest, and reactionary protest at that. It's like, Joe got killed; we're mad. You could go back to 1955 and '60 with the civil rights movement and see that.

Right now, you got to look at things like fusion centers. Fusion centers are the federal government, the state government, and the local municipalities working together to control uprisings.[4] They're so sophisticated now, they turn spontaneous rebellion into parties, into carnivals and festivals.

One example is up on Pennsylvania North, there was an angry mob of a couple thousand people at Freddie Gray's memorial service after his funeral. They called it the Baltimore Uprising. But the next day, it turned into a carnival, so the anger was contained. The federal government was there in terms of military armament, equipment, and helicopters. But they turned it into a celebration by bringing out the church dancers, the young ladies with short skirts, the martial artists to do Capoeira, by bringing out the cultural nationalist drummers. They put community groups in front of the police to face down the community with the claim, "If we let you get to the police, they'll beat you up. We're protecting you."

In reality, they're protecting the police — it's fusion. You have to look at it as hundreds of years of governments dealing with insurrections, mass uprisings, rebellions. They've brought it to a sophisticated science.

PAUL: What do you think of the Black Lives platform?

EDDIE: I'm comfortable with it. It's pretty much a take-off of the Black Panther Party program. But it'll have no substance if there's no building. Even though it talks anti-misogynist theory, anti-imperialism — all that language — it still seems to be a Black nationalist capitalist kind of thing that says, "Put us in charge; let us have the money and the resources. We'll make your lives better." To me, it seems to fall short of addressing the need for a collective, co-operative action among us.

PAUL: I want to make a small difference here, because I think what we're seeing *is* a movement. The simultaneous and spontaneous formations of people arising all over the country have to be looked at as a movement. It's not developed; it's not necessarily a movement like the Black Panther Party, which was an organization inside of a movement. But if we think back to the day, there were, across the country, all kinds of organizations that worked in a similar fashion to the Black Panther Party. That's what movements do. It's similar to the civil rights movement. There were these spread-out organizations across the country.

I'm also going to contrast that decentralized nature — more a feminine nature — of the Black Lives movement to the Black Panther Party, which has a very masculine image. "Do what I say or I'll knock you upside your head," macho thing. Even the women got into that, you know. What's going on now is more of a cooperative, "We don't need you as our leader" thing. That has to be studied, because it replicates itself in so many different places.

EDDIE: I will accept that. That's one of the things I saw in Brazil. Seven thousand young people came together for this celebration in Brazil, the Popular Uprising of Youth.[5] I have never seen so many men in dresses, right? The young people were so great. It was, "I got your back," and "I got your back, too." I said, "God this is amazing."

I can see microcosms of that here in North America. It's not just Black Lives Matter; it's a movement into the future for young people. So I'll accept that. I guess what I was saying was, I expect at some point that a political formation will come out of it that will have more consistency, like the Black Panthers. But it will be all of those things, because that's a movement. I do accept that.

PAUL: I'm challenging you about this because, in fact, the dominant model may need to be matrilineal. Now, trust me — *trust me:* I'm still the guy that Marty Walker and them used to jump on for calling them "chicks." [*Laughter*] Marty was an activist with us and was always present on Eddie's case. But she got so pissed.

So I don't have that matrilineal thing. What I do have is examples of patrilineal domination. Then I look at matrilineal energy. Seriously. If you want stuff done, you go to Black women; you don't go to Black men. It was the same way in the Party. Women were the backbone of that organization. It's women, period, who move things in a much, much more cooperative way, even when they're imitating patrilineal structures. You think about ancient societies, the right of kinship passed through the woman.

EDDIE: I would use different descriptions, because this hierarchical structure, where you have the Big Leader, and then the followers, can be useful. As opposed to a horizontal structure where you have networks.

Horizontal organizing is good because it's inclusive. But somewhere along the line, in order for horizontal structures to be effective, there's got to be some general consensus of what the boundaries are, of what you can and can't do. That hierarchical structure said, for instance, "No smoking dope until you're off duty." The horizontal structure says, "Do whatever you want to do." There's got to be some major change in both for it all to be operational.

But I think women have always been undervalued. Women kept us alive, not just in the Black Panther Party, but the civil rights movement, the Marcus Garvey Back to Africa movement. Men get the talking-head recognition. That's been a problem; men want to listen to issues from other men, when the actual structures are viable because of women. Even though Elaine Brown ran whole programs, when you looked up on the stage and saw the Support Committee, it was primarily men.

That's on men to deal with. You know, we don't get free until we all free.

So Many People to Admire

PAUL: I don't define myself as a revolutionary, but I do have a peculiar passion, and that is for Black, self-trained historians. These are people who spent a lot of time outside the academy but made, in my mind, significant contributions. Like Dr. Elinor [Des Verney] Sinnette. Dr. Sinnette was one of the people I decided to make my mentor as I kept studying. My mentors just happened; they were usually women, usually much older. Nothing formal, I just claim them as being strong influences on me.

Elinor Sinnette wrote a great dissertation, the first full biography on Arthur Schomburg. Schomburg was himself a great bibliophile and a self-trained historian.

So in my thirties, after I finished library school, I end up working as an acquisitions librarian at Moorland-Spingarn Research Center at Howard University. Who do I meet on the first day but Elinor Sinnette. We were immediately sharing information, and as we talked, I realized she was the woman that Penelope Bullock, my mentor in Atlanta, had told me about. Penelope Bullock was also a very acute, self-trained historian. A badass woman.

When I say badass woman, I mean in library school, they teach you to put together what they call pathfinders. A pathfinder is a bibliography that lists all the sources one might use to research a particular subject. Dr. Bullock was the specialist who put together what would be the equivalent of a pathfinder of pathfinders for the study of African American history. They didn't have electronic databases at the time she did this, so everything was the books. I mean you got to *know* that stuff backwards and forwards, man. A lot of it I knew, so we could talk. She'd say, "Mr. Coates, that is brilliant. But have you considered . . ."

See, you're stuck on *"brilliant,"* but she's asking you something. Not because she knows; not because you did something wrong. She's asking because it occurred to her — but it didn't occur to *me.*

"No. I didn't think about that."

Damn. Why didn't I, you know? Penelope Bullock was a great inspiration in my life, a great model.

She liked that I focused on uncovering the works of early, self-trained historians. And that I wanted to publish those works.

This is a whole group of women and men who just don't get credit. Like Drusilla Dunjee Houston. She was a journalist and historian, and had about a grade-school education. She and a whole mess of people who worked to preserve Black history are considered historians without a portfolio. Doc Ben [Yosef Alfredo Antonio Ben-Jochannan] was pretty much self-trained. Now, in his case he worked inside and outside of the academy. Doc Ben had quite a bit of schooling, he just didn't have as much as he claimed. Still, by the time he died, he had connected the Nile Valley to Black history like no one before him.

One of the baddest guys these days is Dr. Charles Finch, down in Atlanta. He's retired now, a medical doctor and highly educated. He's no different than many of the great older European historians — because none of *them* were "historians," they just wrote history. They applied a particular method, not necessarily a scientific method, to their studies. These days, most Black historians who come along, even those who are self-trained, have a ton of college behind them.

Gosh, there's so many people to admire. In terms of Black publishers, Haki Madhubuti probably stands at the top for me. Haki's Third World Press is eleven years older than Black Classic Press, and when I was putting BCP together, I had them as a model. But I also had others. There was a press called Ahidiana-Habari. There was Jihad Press, which was out of Newark, run by Amiri Baraka. There was the East in Brooklyn. They all went by the way.

When BCP started, there were presses in England that I became aware of. Bogle L'Ouverture Press was one. Then New Beacon Books with John La Rose from Trinidad was one I admired. John died a few years ago but Sarah White, his wife, continues the store. Glenn Thompson, who's gone now, who started the Writers and Readers Publishing Cooperative, was someone I admired very much. But Third World Press, through all kinds of adversity, has managed to stay.

There's also a lot of booksellers to admire. Booksellers and presses, they represent a contained, collective consciousness. All of these people were contributing to creating a voice within the Black community. It was a way of resisting.

In terms of admiring small press versus mainstream publishing, I don't think either is inherently bad or good. It's possible to carry a strong message through the commercial press, and a strong message through

Black independent publishers. But you have to ask how you want to be a part of that message.

For example, Haki has published every book he's written, and he has a strong following in the Black community, which is the community he's concerned with. Now, would he have been as strong if he had published with a white press? He would have had more white readers, but his message was geared to the Black community. The Black press goes closer to the root, closer to the actual message. It's driven by people's daily experience.

Then you have someone like Baldwin. If James Baldwin had been limited to the Black community, his voice wouldn't be known to the world — and his voice definitely had to be known to the world.

In mainstream publishing, Toni Morrison was just awesome in terms of publishing and getting voices out there. Before she started writing, herself, she edited a ton of books for people like Muhammad Ali, who wrote *The Greatest.* She edited Angela Davis's autobiography. She was hip, she was really good. And how could I talk about publishing and writing without mentioning Walter Mosley?

Of course, I admire my son, Ta-Nehisi, for

248

following in the steps of people like Walter — and understanding that he's following people like that. So I got a lot of people to admire.

Little Things like Cutting the Grass

EDDIE: I still wake up at three in the morning. For decades, the guards woke us up at 3:00 a.m. to count us. My biorhythm is that I wake up; I don't even have to look at a clock. I'm still trying to figure out how to adjust that.

All during my years inside, I and people like me were bringing in people from the outside to help, to teach people. But I don't think it had much impact. Over my forty-four years inside, I honestly didn't see any big change in consciousness. People paid attention to Rodney King and the riots as the reactions to police brutality. People watched all this stuff on the news, but it didn't change their consciousness, I believe. People in prison were angry. Anger, frustration — most of it was about, "How much money can we make?" But it's funny. Even a few years out of prison, I'm still very connected to the guys inside. I just mailed a guy in prison a bunch of photos last night. This guy is one of the organizers of Friend of a Friend. So in various ways I do stuff to help them.

I think I've always had faith in humans. Ideologically, I'm an international revolutionary socialist, and I've always had faith that if people understand enough and if they work together — it might take hundreds of years — they will eventually develop the kind of society that will be healthy and good for everybody. If the planet can live that long.

I've always had faith, even faith in people who other people write off, "Oh, don't waste your time on them." I guess that's my belief in the universal creator. There's this positive energy, and there's negative energy, and we have to figure out how to use both in a good way.

When I first got to prison as a Black Panther, I was agnostic. Then, probably about five years later, the Muslim thing swept the movement. So I became a Sunni Muslim, and I was active for about five years. Then, for about three years, outside the Sunni community, I continued to practice Ramadan.

I studied Christianity, and I studied Islam, and I tinkered with Buddhism a little, and at some point, I realized: OK, everybody's saying the same thing but they're saying it from their perspective. Which means: We're right and everybody else is wrong. We are all going to Nirvana or heaven or paradise, and all *you* all is going to hell.

I said, "OK, humans and human-made religion are using this stuff in their own interest, to control people. You can militarily conquer people but you can't control them unless you can conquer them spiritually."

So I recognize the universality of the spirit, but not manmade stuff. I think that over my period of learning and struggling and trying to know about the different religions, I came to the conclusion: Take humanity out of the equation; take "Man's" construct out. What's left is that everybody's born with universal goodwill and good peace. Of course, then we train it out of people and cause them to lose it.

I have two sons, you know. Ronald and Deshawn. Certainly, my relationship with my children has changed since I got out. I can go see them now, I can interact with my sons and my grandchildren, and that's a hundred percent improvement. They actually love me.

Right now, my sense of home is over on Tioga Parkway, the house where I live. The house Paul provided for me. No matter where I go — it's weird, cause I want to go places all the time — I always miss home. I always want to come back there.

Unfortunately, I have to worry about little things like cutting the grass. I was looking at it this morning and telling myself, "Everybody else is cutting their grass. I'm going to have to get somebody money to do it, or I'm going to have to get out there, myself."

Which is a simple little thing, but it's important. It's not just ownership, it's like being part of the community.

We Are, and We Always Have Been

PAUL: You have to remember that very, very much a part of the process of slavery, very much a part of Jim Crow, and a part of the containment of Black people around the world today is to embed them in their own enslavement. There's no future after that. Black people in and after enslavement were raised into that. I was raised into that. Children today are raised into it, because those old ideas linger on.

But how is it that David Walker, a Black man in 1829, has it in his mind to collect together fragments of history and use those fragments to lay out "David Walker's Appeal," his political manifesto? This becomes one of the early, grounded historical documents that talks about Blacks as being higher than slaves.

David Walker uses a lot of the Bible to connect these fragments. My fascination is with him, but it's also in the fact that there was a conversation going on then that he became a part of; it wasn't that he was talking only from himself. He was part of a conversation going against the mainstream that said, "Niggers ain't shit."

There was this counter-conversation among Black people, saying, "We exist. Yes, we are. And we always have been."

That narrative never got lost. It was always there but got suppressed. So think about someone who carries that narrative, who carries it into print: I see that person as a freedom fighter. I see them carrying the word, delivering the *word* as a freedom fighter.

They're resisting the thing that's stronger than chains: They're resisting control of the mind. These writers do that. Many of them are called propagandists — because they want Black people to know their history, so they can't be enslaved again.

They believe this education they carry is the most potent weapon, and usually, their lives show actions that support what they put into print. I look on that work as being as powerful as anything that Nat Turner did, anything Denmark Vesey did, anything the ancestors who resisted did. Writing is just as powerful. This is a missing part of that quilt we call American history. The fact that it's in books, and the fact that it's still unknown, calls me into action. I have a duty and a responsibility to make this Black history known. So for me this is a sacred act.

I was just interviewed by some folks at CSPAN. I talked about how the baddest historian of them all was a Black woman. Her name was Drusilla Dunjee Houston. She wrote in 1926. The interviewer said, "Yes, but does that history still stand up?"

I told him, "No history stands up. All history gets criticized."[6]

There are mistakes with whatever historian you go to. Many people, dealing with Herodotus, the so-called father of history, tear his work apart. But Herodotus assumes a responsibility to tell the story of the world's people as he encounters them. There's a narrative, a truth he lays out that ties it together. It's the same with almost anybody writing history. The same with Drusilla Dunjee Houston, who wrote *Wonderful Ethiopians of the Ancient Cushite Empire.* I'm on my soapbox now . . .

Why impose such a burden on someone

who is making such an effort to tell history? It's not as important that her book stand up as it is her efforts — what it cost her to write that book in the first place. What does it mean that you're a Black woman, in the middle of Oklahoma — the Negro territories in the early 1920s? What causes you to write about the heroic deeds of Black people who lived thousands of years ago in Africa?

She made herself the one responsible for pulling this stuff from what she called, "the dry bones of history." Why isn't white America doing that? Why aren't other Black people doing that? Inside of her actions is a tale of the history of this country.

I've lived for the past forty-plus years with the responsibility to make these stories known. Now, I'm looking to how to pass this stuff on. At the same time, I still have knowledge to contribute. Like when it comes to self-trained historians, I'm still probably one of the more knowledgeable people in this country. I'm sure there are some young cats coming along that have built on the stuff we've laid out. They probably know more than I know. But I'm still in a position to make knowledge available and to build a body of that literature.

You know, I've talked about Black Classic

Press, but I really think BCP Digital Printing, which began in 1995, is probably my most significant contribution. The printing helps keep the doors open.

When Eddie and I started planning things, back in the George Jackson Prison Movement, the first part of the plan was to open a bookstore. The second part was a publishing company. The third part was the printing company — and I had no idea at the time how that was going to manifest itself. It has, though.

I think about all Black publishing companies and, great as they were, none of them printed books because it was so difficult. BCP has done it now for over twenty years. It's been hard; we haven't thrived. But I'm proud that the printing generates support from other publishers and money for Black Classic Press. All that, my dear — all that has really been a challenge for this brother.

Remembering Howard

Howard Reed was a constant presence in Eddie's life, though, over the years, he and Eddie had less and less in common. Howard's life was his own and his story remains untold. Yet Howard perhaps stands as an example of those of us in radical movements who remain on the sidelines — and a reminder of the toll that white supremacy can exact on the human psyche, even without the infliction of a prison sentence.

EDDIE: My buddy Howard Reed just died. Howard, who'd been my childhood friend, since before I went in the army. After I got back home, he was in bad shape. He had AIDS, but he was still getting around. His feet would swell up. I guess he had gout also.

Howard had been a truck driver the whole time I had been in prison, so he wasn't impoverished, but he wasn't doing too well. Right after I got out of jail, I got him medical stuff and a heating pad. I hung out with him. He was driving and would come get me.

He was so bitter. Back when I joined the Panthers, he had decided not to join. All of us talking about joining, and he was like, "Uhhhh . . . No." But he had always been a Black-talker. Always talking Black, but never willing to do anything.

When I came back out, Howard was still talking Black, but now it was, "We'd be free if it wasn't for them niggers." Still not doing anything.

I had him over to my house once, when a bunch of young people was also there. The young people and I are talking politics and doing PE [political education]. I invited him into the room, come on in. So he's setting there and he starts groaning about, "We'll never be free, we can't be free, we can't do anything, we don't have no unity, we fight each other . . ."

Finally, I say, "You need to get out." I actually had to put him out of the house.

I think I might have gone over to his house one time after that or maybe he came back over to my house. And then he died.

Howard was bitter because he had never done anything, you know. But he knew a lot of stuff. Apparently, he had really studied. Like, you can run into some junkies that know so much. They go and get high, but they can still tell you all these facts, like when Ethiopia was in charge of Egypt . . . Howard was one of those people. Knew a lot; never did anything.

It was sad — but I wouldn't have made no difference in his life. By the time I came back, he was on his last leg.

CHAPTER 13:
THAT NEXT CHAPTER:
A RETROSPECTIVE

An autumn afternoon in Baltimore, in Eddie Conway's office at The Real News Network. The general affect is amiable, scattered, politically engaged. There's a desk, stacks of papers, a couple of chairs, a slightly worn couch. On the walls, a picture of the revolutionary, Assata Shakur, a sign about an old Black Panther Party "Free Food Program," an updated 1971 print by Panther artist Emory Douglas of a Black woman shouting/singing/crying "Hallelujah!" Over in the corner several boxes of clothes are ready for distribution at the Sandtown-Winchester projects in West Baltimore.

Eddie leans comfortably back behind his desk in a swivel chair. Paul Coates sits nearby, on a battered office chair.

EDDIE: How would I sum up my friendship with Paul? I don't know if I should rag on Paul. He's an old man. What I do remember was, "This guy's like me. Serious, like I'm serious." Because I'd been dealing with so many knuckleheads, for want of a better terminology. I don't know when our first encounter happened, but I felt like, "OK, I can work with this guy."

PAUL: He said that so nice. I feel like saying something nice back about him. But my memory was I didn't like him much. [*Eddie's laughing*] Like I've said before, Eddie was exerting his Panther-ness, you know — and I didn't like that. But we didn't see each other much before he was incarcerated.

The moment he went to jail, it was "brother." We could hear each other, we could talk to each other. I never had to worry about him not being his word. A lot of joy came out of that. He was my comrade — that was absolutely the bonding thing — he was my comrade.

Probably what he's taught me the most is the ability to keep going — just to keep going. I'd visit him and he'd be, "Hey man, what's up?"

I knew it was hard; every day it was hard, but Eddie had an ability not to drape that on me. He wasn't trying to put pounds on me as I walked out the door. His dealing with incarceration in a way that made our visits *about our visits* always fascinated me. I don't think I could do that. The other piece is his charismatic self, and his ability to speak to even the crazies in a nice manner. Whereas, I'm saying, "Get the fuck away from me," in every language I can.

We were out at some rally recently [*starts laughing*], and this guy — General Whatever-the-Hell-His-Name-Is — I mean he actually thinks he's a general because he was in the Black Panther Party for three months or something? Eddie was talking to him, but I'm saying, "Nawww . . ."

EDDIE: He had three stars, an air horn, Navy Seal jacket.

PAUL: Every time he got a chance at the mic, he was saying, "You all need to follow me!" Eddie was talking to him real respectful. That's how he does people. That's part of his charisma.

EDDIE: [*Eddie's laughing, too*] Red, black, and green, right? An ex-Panther?

PAUL: But look, I think it's important not to be afraid of saying negative things about the Panthers. Because the Panther Party has moved into a degree of myth. Things that are bad about the Party just don't get discussed. The Free Breakfast Program, and how many bags of food we gave away, etcetera, gets the attention. That's myth-making.

EDDIE: Yeah. Romanticizing the whole thing. That's what I tell people. To look at the Panthers and think it was a beautiful thing is OK. But know that underneath, there was pain and suffering and sorrow and poverty and hunger and all the rest.

Like, Paul, we went out to that Fiftieth Anniversary of the Black Panther Party in Oakland [2016], right? Would you say that anything got resolved there about CO-INTELPRO and all that government surveillance?

PAUL: None of that happened. Not in a substantial way.

EDDIE: Yeah. You had an anniversary, a reunion.[1] There were workshops and discussions about where we've been or where we are now, but this was not political. "Come and eat the fried chicken. See how many of your comrades are still alive. And make sure you don't beat each other up."

PAUL: What you're saying is very true. Think of it like a family reunion. You're not going to litigate about how you-know-who got what when they shouldn'ta got it. You might say behind their back, "So and so's always got away with stuff and they still do." But you're not going to bring it up to so-and-so.

EDDIE: Right now, though, the important thing for me is telling our stories. Giving a voice to people that have no voice.

PAUL: For me, it's my grandchildren. I spent a lot of time thinking outward, you know, of Black people. And now I'm blessed that I have the opportunity and the health to work with, once again, some hardheaded boys. I got the girls, too, but the girls are not hardheaded. I have an opportunity to influence them all in a way that they can go on and change the world.

There was an incident when one of my grandsons jumped a turnstile in DC. It was very, very disappointing. I know he has a lot of promise, but at the same time, it's an opportunity to talk to him — for about an hour? [*Laughs*]

I'm talking about that one incident, but really it's about how he carries himself in the world, his impact on other people, his consideration for his mother, for his uncles, for himself. The power of his embarrassment and making him see that people are not proud of him. How important is that lesson?

I'm telling him, "You will write this up, acknowledge what you did and its impact on other people in your life." Of course, I had my other grandson there, listening to this. So I switch over to the other one, who's thinking this is not about him. I say, "I want you to do this, too, about your schoolwork, because you're being an idiot there, much in the same way."

I'm still going to publish books. I'm going to deal with that Black consciousness out there, but joy? Is being able to be with these kids up close. Not trying to make up for what I did as a father, but doing it maybe a little different. A little less uptight, a little less thinking that the world was going to end if I didn't get it right. I get great joy out of that.

EDDIE: That's what I miss. I miss that whole piece of my life. What you just said about raising kids.

When I was in prison, I had a visit with my son Ronald, maybe once a week, but those visits stopped after a while. Once a week is not enough, so that whole piece — molding and shaping and sharing and learning and growing together — is gone. Losing that is part of the damage of long-term incarceration. It is a piece of genocide — and it's all over the Black community. Check out that definition of genocide in the United Nations Charter.[2] That's one of the pieces, yeah.

So I'm still learning to be a grandparent. It's not easy, and part of the damage of prison is that it makes you self-contained. You're self-centered, whether you like it or not — "I got this; I'm good." You're in your own world, so it's hard to reach out and share. But that's what being a parent, or grandparent, means. That's something I'm learning.

Let me say this, too. All that time I did was hard time, you know. Every day — you know this — every day you do inside is hard time. I had so many other people inside relying on me as an example. I had to carry that hard time on my shoulders. I'm surprised, in fact, when people, who are not political or not spiritual, don't do drugs, don't drink, or do everything they can do to escape, do their time. It's hard to do hard time on a natural. You're always facing that reality.

PAUL: But with all of that, Eddie never made me feel like it was my responsibility to get him out of there. Never.

EDDIE: I want to add something to Paul, now. You know, I thought I was smart when I came back from Europe and joined the Panther Party. I thought I knew what was going on. But what I learned from Paul over the years — and this wasn't an easy thing — was critical thinking.

To realize that I wasn't smart at all, but to realize that I didn't have to be. I just had to know how to find out the things I wanted to know, 'cause I couldn't know everything. Conversation after conversation with Paul, I would over-generalize and look at the surface. And Paul would say, "Well, yeah, part of that's good. But the piece I take from that . . ." He would make me look at things differently. So, over the years — and I'm still a student, I'm still working on it — I developed a way of looking at stuff a lot more critical.

But the other piece I take away is honest, righteous love for somebody. I couldn't have had a biological brother like Paul — I mean, this is the brother you would choose, you know? So a piece of him and me is loyalty, but a piece of it is integrity.

PAUL: Mm-hmm. That's the piece I'm speaking back to you. To sit in front of somebody and to know that that person is not going to lie to you. It's invaluable. It draws you in further, and that's a bond. An immeasurable bond.

Even though we don't hang out much these days. This guy disses me all the time. I have to say, "Hey man, can I get on your schedule?"

EDDIE: Naw, his schedule is just as bad. He was an hour late getting here, that's evidence.

PAUL: Yeah. We'll definitely reach out and talk, but we won't do it every day. I just know he's going somewhere, doing something. Every day he does that — every day he's out here living this new life — he is fulfilling on a promise that he and I made to so many people.

"When Eddie comes out, he's going to be a force of good in our community."

I can hear myself saying that over and over. I have seen so many people come out of jail and *not* do it, so there's relief and there's joy. There's also a great freedom for me.

I just never knew how much Eddie being

in jail shaped my life. There really isn't a Paul Coates without a Black Classic Press. That's my life, and if I'm to be remembered outside my family, it's that. Well, there isn't a Black Classic Press without Eddie. The press was conceived inside of a commitment to Eddie and other political prisoners, so now, I get to look at that. It's not like I'm looking at him dead in the ground and saying, "It's closure." This is closure where you go on to the next chapter. And Eddie's writing that next chapter.

He and I argue sometimes. Like about organizing events, whether there should be a fried chicken dinner, or whether the coffee is being brewed *correctly*. We bump heads, because we're both strong personalities. It doesn't matter; Eddie's just crazy. [*Laughter*]

EDDIE: It's funny. I was sifting through that as he was talking, right? There was certainly tremendous pain in the prison. There was that experience of not being able to go to your mama's funeral, not being able to watch your kids and nieces and nephews grow up. There was pain of having that door shut on you all the time. But the day I walked in, I walked in working. And the day I walked out, I walked out working. There was never any disconnect from who I was. It's just a relief that that cage is not here.

So yeah. I guess now I'm working on that next chapter.

was never any disconnect from who I was. It's just to tell that their rage is not here. So years, I guess now I'm working on the next chapter.

CHAPTER 14:
NO ANGELS OF HISTORY
COMING TO SAVE US

People carry around so much history. These days, activists and revolutionaries — people who love the world so much that they have devoted their lives to the prospect of sharing it equally — can get lost inside all the newly released historical accounts of revolutionary groups like the Panthers. Reading books, watching documentaries, we wonder: Did they get this right? Where was I? Is this how we go down in history?

But over the years, it's our lives among our people — however we define "our people" — our love and competition and feuds and reconciliations that give history its texture, and a reality that scores of studies, however informative, can only hint at.

I am not an activist or revolutionary. I do not come from any "organized Left." I am a journalist who, on assignment one day in November 1988, went to the DC Jail to interview four of the women in the "Capitol bombing case." It was there that I met Laura White-horn, and there that the spirit of this book began to form.

There were actually seven "Capitol bomb-ing" defendants, fighting in what they preferred to call the Resistance Conspiracy Case. One had skipped bail. The four remaining women and two men, all white and varying degrees of middle-class, awaited trial on charges of car-rying out a series of 1980s property bomb-ings. Designed to call out egregious US poli-cies, the explosions — including the 1983 bombing outside the Senate chamber in the Capitol Building — killed or injured no one.

Somehow, I had come here from another world to these people, who, claiming resi-dence in some unknown, obstinate dimension, wanted to be called political prisoners.

Laura was one of a comparatively few white organizers — the media labeled them "self-avowed revolutionaries" — who'd spent years working to support Puerto Rican, Indigenous, and African American liberation movements. She was and is still on board with every point of the original Black Panther Party Ten Point Program. To our great and lasting surprise, we fell in love and into a relationship that continues to this day.

When Laura was first locked up, in the women's section of the Baltimore City Jail,

Eddie had already been in prison for fifteen years. Alone, away from her codefendants, Laura got support from people inside who were sure that she and Eddie must have some kind of bond. Laura had definitely heard of Eddie and, over the years, he heard occasional mention of Laura Whitehorn, too.

Released in 1999, Laura ended up serving over fourteen years in federal prison. Today, she openly admits to having done (most of) the things she was charged with. Soon after she got off parole, Laura was in Baltimore, where Dominque Stevenson arranged for her to go to the Jessup Correctional Institute to visit Eddie. And so it was that Laura Whitehorn — unashamedly guilty of having bombed the Capitol — later took me to meet Eddie Conway — almost certifiably innocent of having shot a police officer.

A lot has happened since Eddie got out. In July 2018, he and Dominque were married. They still live on Tioga Parkway in Paul's old house, though they talk of someday moving to New Orleans. Besides their separate jobs, they share a few projects, one of which is the Tubman House, which works to bring self-determination to Baltimore's Sandtown-Winchester community. Friend of a Friend is also doing well.

Paul lives with his wife, Rosalyn Wilcots

Coates, in Washington, DC. Black Classic Press, still going strong, celebrated its fortieth anniversary in May 2018. With his recent marriage, Paul has added two children to his crew of seven, Darius and Jared.

In Baltimore, on March 7, 2019, various activists, artists, and Panther communities all crowded into Red Emma's Bookstore and Café to help Eddie celebrate his fifth anniversary outside. March 7 also marked Eddie's first official day off parole. Laura and I came down from New York City to join people from Baltimore and all over the country, most of whom had spent years working for Eddie's release and keeping his name alive.

Emory Douglas, artist for the original Panther newspaper, whose art continues to fascinate and inspire, is here from the Bay Area. One in a long line of speakers, his tribute is short and to the point:

Much love to you Eddie, comrade over fifty years. Thank you. Much love and appreciation.

Eddie's lawyer, Bob Boyle, is also here from New York:

I met Eddie around 1992. He sat down, put his arms on the table and said, "So.

Are you gonna get me outta here?" It took a while. Sometimes it's hard to believe, but thanks to all of you, we can be here tonight. . . .

Several cultural workers also speak. One is Mama Rashida, who has taken her theater inside prisons with Friend of a Friend. There are performances by poets and musicians and a local Baltimore rapper, Son of Nun. John Duda, a cofounder of Red Emma's, tells us that he learned about Eddie when he moved to Baltimore, because people there refused to let the struggle to free him die out:

The first time I talked to Eddie on the phone, I was super-nervous. I expected some sort of superhero or revolutionary angel — who was this person who'd endured so much and fought so hard? But what that conversation taught me was that Eddie is a guy. He's a wonderful, amazing, super-brave, super-smart, super-committed guy. But he's ultimately just a dude — like the rest of us? That's really the lesson, that there are no heroes, no angels of history coming to save us. It's just people making choices.

Of course, Laura gets called up to speak:

274

So after my arrest, I got to the Baltimore City Jail, which was the pits of the pits, and I started getting all these kites from guys in the men's prison, saying, "You must know Eddie Conway, so I'm sending you pages from some law books so you can fight your case." I'm thinking, "No law will help me. I'm fucked. It's over . . ."

Of course, I'd heard of Eddie. I first knew his name because of you, who fought for him. One of the things about Eddie is that, first, he's honest; he never gives you bullshit. Also, Eddie expresses what a political prisoner is, which is not necessarily someone who suffers more than anyone else. We know, inside prison, everyone suffers. People who suffer the most are those whose names no one on the outside knows. So it's not because you're invigorated by suffering; it's because you never stopped doing the work.

Suddenly, Paul Coates yells out from the audience, "Tell Us What You Did!" Laura answers:

You don't ask people that. [*Laughter*] . . . My comrades and I were underground, the United States gave us many opportunities to protest, and there were lots of very good targets. My personal favorite is we bombed the Patrolmen's Benevolent Association in New York and Israeli Aircraft Industry offices in solidarity with Palestine. . . . The one that got us in the most trouble is the Capitol, which we bombed after the US invaded Grenada to overthrow the first Black socialist country in this hemisphere. But today, we drove past the Capitol and I said, "That looks OK. I don't know what the problem is."

It was the Panthers and the Black liberation movement that gave me a sense of how to change the things I hated in this country and what human beings can be. You gave me that, Eddie.

Dominque, who was instrumental in organizing this event, says only a little:

I wish he could stop and retire, but then that's just me as a wife . . .

Malik Rahim steps up. In 1971, inside the Orleans Parish prison, he changed the life of Albert Woodfox by introducing him to the Black Panther Party. This was just before Woodfox was sent to Angola, where, with Herman Wallace and Robert King, he became one of the Angola Three, set up for the murder of a prison guard. Like, Laura, Malik Rahim first met Eddie when Dominque took him to visit at Jessup.

I cannot tell you how, at some low points of my life, Eddie and Dominque touched my spirit. We have a saying: "Every time an elder make his transition without passing down his life experiences to the next generation, a library has just burned down."

Eddie, I hope you live to see one hundred. But I know one thing: when you make your transition, you won't be on that list of libraries burning down. All power to the people.

By now, it is way past Paul Coates's turn to speak:

You all here: I don't know if you're present to it, but you are witnessing a miracle. Not only that five years ago, Eddie gets out of jail. But he gets a job at The Real News — that just don't happen. Eddie gets out of jail, gets a job, and has a beautiful wife waiting for him. WHO DOES THAT?

When Eddie was in jail, one of the strongest arguments we hung was that we can't wait to get him back into the community so he can organize. You can find that on the old flyers. You see that, over and over. There was a period when even Eddie was shaking his head on whether he was coming out of there. But he come out, faithful to the same principles that he went in with. The first thing I said to him was, "Look brother, you need to take a break. Lay off for two weeks." Did he listen to me? He was down at Gilmor Homes the next day.

I knew I would ramble around a bit. There's so much in this room and in this moment. Because Eddie is so central to my life. I'm doing some thinking and writing now, and Eddie comes up quite a bit. You see, when you talk about forty years of Black Classic Press, you actually go back to Eddie's incarceration and my leaving the Black Panther Party, around '71, '72. I had gone to Oakland to get support. We didn't get support and I was thrown out of the Party. . . . Eddie said fuck them, and that's the way we rolled . . .

I owe quite a bit of my life to Eddie Conway. Because of him being who he said he was and because I never had a reason to doubt him. So I thank you, brother, I'm just so happy that you get to live your life with your wife — and maybe you'll listen to her and chill out some. But if you don't, it's OK, too. You're still my brother.

It must be hard to face up to all this, but somehow, Eddie manages it:

I wouldn't be standing here without this support. The whole forty-four years, communities, white, Black, Brown, straight, gay, young and old, came out, struggled, rallied, campaigned, sent postcards. . . . I thank everybody, even if your support was just in your heart or your mind or your spirit.

Because I work at The Real News, I'm forced to say something. The world is changing fast, and not for the better. When I got out of prison, I was exhausted. I said, "I've done forty-four years; I worked with thousands of guys inside prison, worked with hundreds of programs. I gave at the office." I wanted to go lay out on the beach. I had friends that had jobs and could have fixed it so I wouldn't have to go to work.

But I traveled down the streets of Baltimore and I saw conditions had changed so that there was no way I could go to the beach. There was no way I could not get involved in helping change things for our young people, for our old people. When we organized in the late '60s and '70s, we organized because conditions were really bad. That's why the Panthers came into being. Fifty years later, conditions are ten times worse.

If I have any effect on people here at all, I'm saying this: Do your little part. Do whatever you can do to help change these conditions. Because we're moving into a critical period of history, not for just poor and oppressed people, Black people, but for humanity itself. So you need to engage. Do whatever little bit you can, but you need to do something.

That being said, the celebration continues. Eddie and Paul continue. Actually, there being over two million human beings remaining inside US jails and prisons — and a fearsome global swing to the white-supremacist right — that "struggle" continues, too.

AFTERWORD:
INSIDE EDDIE CONWAY'S STORY IS SO MUCH BLACK HISTORY

Over the decades, Paul took his son Ta-Nehisi to visit Eddie many times. But the first time Ta-Nehisi met Eddie was when he was a baby, brought to a prison visit by his mother, Cheryl Waters, whom Ta-Nehisi credits with "giving me the tools to be a writer." Later, as it turned out, Eddie himself came to play a pivotal role in Ta-Nehisi's writing.

An essential element in Ta-Nehisi's work today comes from those prison visits. Five years after Eddie's release from prison, Ta-Nehisi talked to me about what he remembers of Eddie Conway, the Black Panthers, the US government's infiltration of the Panther Party, and how the FBI's Counterintelligence Program has impacted his family. All of this led to Ta-Nehisi's sense — way before he could write — that resistance can be its own reward.

In some profound sense, I was born into jail. Visiting Eddie Conway in the Maryland

Penitentiary is one of the earliest things I remember. I was very young, maybe four, but stuff would strike me, like metal gates, mechanized, moving bars that you went through. I remember realizing that Eddie couldn't leave this place, and he didn't have things that we had. It's a radicalizing experience at that young age, seeing somebody in prison. It marks you.

We visited as a regular thing, so I used to get bored a lot, too. "What are we doing here? What are we talking about?"

See, my dad had been in something called the Black Panther Party. He's very proud of having been a Panther, but he has this aversion — not to activism, but to being an activist himself. And yet he's maintained the concept of struggle. You always had to struggle. You couldn't not be about struggle. That was something that was put in me.

The way things ended with my dad and the Panther Party left him with a bad taste. There was the split in the national Party. He was also very upset at the end, and felt that the Baltimore political prisoners like Eddie weren't treated appropriately by the Panthers in California. My dad does not tell a triumphant story. He tells a story about the ideals being correct, about a righteous organization. But he also tells the story of a lot of foolishness.

When I was young I didn't see a lot of older folks who had been Panthers. Dad had Baltimore friends, but not friends who identified as Panthers. But sometimes, former BPP people would pop in and out of my life. Afeni Shakur came down to live in Baltimore for a while. I saw her quite a bit with her daughter, Sekyiwa.

I remember Black Classic Press and my dad, stapling books and pamphlets with a saddle-stitch stapler. I worked there all the time — my dad made me work there — I remember not liking it. But there were a lot of books around me as a child, just a ton of books. My dad published Bobby Seale's *Seize the Time,* but I had already read the original before he printed the BCP edition. Same with *The Panther Is a Black Cat.* He had tons of books about the Black Panther Party around the house, a real collection. I read all that stuff.

I was the first of my dad's children to be raised entirely under his codes — which was not fun. We didn't celebrate Christmas and, because my dad would think about *every-thing,* we didn't celebrate Kwanzaa, either. Actually, we didn't celebrate any holiday at all. And for a long time, we didn't eat meat;

couldn't stand for the pledge of allegiance. Sure, it's principled politics, but when you're a child, it's isolating.

Only later — I was about twelve or thirteen; this was the era of Public Enemy — did I come to realize what the Panthers were actually about, what those books were fighting for. I was listening to hip-hop references to Assata Shakur and the Panthers. And I realized: this is my *dad.* I started to read more.

I began to ask my dad questions, and that got us to another relationship level. That was when the piece with Eddie began to cohere, and I began to understand what was going on.

It's funny how these things have an influence on you. Actually, a lot of what I write now reflects some of the concerns in the original Panther Party's Ten Point Program — housing, jobs, land, freedom, education, an end to incarceration. They're things that Black folks have always wanted; I don't consider myself as discovering them. These are the ideas I was exposed to as a very, very young child.

I think there's a link between radical Black movements like the Panthers and the rise of mass incarceration. People who prefer the civil rights movement to militant Black groups will say, "Well, the militants embraced violence, so the state bringing its wrath upon them is no surprise." But I don't think most people realize how deeply all Black people have been criminalized.

Inside Eddie's story is so much Black history. There's a reason there are political prisoners. We do not have a carceral system that is a neutral arbiter, separate from the prejudices and intentions of the state. Folks who take up causes against those prejudices are more likely to end up behind bars for long periods of time. Compare somebody like Eddie Conway with that Bundy family out West. They took over a whole federal wildlife refuge and occupied it for several weeks — and basically got away with it. You couldn't be part of any Black or leftist radical tradition and expect anything like that to happen.[1]

But if you'll notice in my article, "The Case for Reparations," I actually focus on middle- and working-class Black people, not militants.[2] What I'm trying to do is take this country at its word. The point is that the entire bargain is corrupt. Even if Black people listen to and do exactly what we're supposed to do, it doesn't work. We've tried that before. Those Black people who lived by society's dictates on how they should conduct themselves were not immune from the violence of the state. Martin Luther King's nonviolence did not sate J. Edgar Hoover's wrath at all. Ultimately, it was kind of irrelevant what Huey Newton or what my dad were about.

A few years ago, I went on Henry Louis Gates's TV show, *Finding Your Roots*. My dad was there for the filming, and Gates had found my dad's FBI file. Not just the file; he'd also found a report from the Baltimore field office to Hoover, asking permission to foment division between the Panthers in California and my dad. Gates had a letter, in which Hoover presumably gave his permission to target my dad, saying basically, "I want something done with this dude."[3]

When you have something like that in your immediate family, you just don't have the luxury and distance and faith to believe that the system has checks and balances that will prevent the worst. It breeds a kind of skepticism, man — to put it lightly. It's no mistake that I am who I am and I write what I write. At the core of everything I write is the fact that I don't like bullies. I think I got that from my dad.

■ ■ ■ ■

I haven't written about political cases much because we're in this era of mass incarceration. That's been my focus, because most people in prison never had a choice. For them, it's not like, "I got radicalized so I decided to oppose the ways this country conducts itself . . ." Should we differentiate those who take a stand — a worthy stand against injustice — and those who are just trying to breathe? It's no mistake that where Freddie Gray came from was the most incarcerated zip code in the state. Our people are born into lives in which prison is almost predetermined.

That's partly why my dad's work, over more than forty years, has been to provide books for Black folks. To make sure they have the tools they need to understand the world they're living in. He don't have to depend on nobody; he don't have to deal with politics. His work still affects me. It's made me supportive of movements today, like Black Lives Matter. But I also feel like my dad probably feels — on a personal level, it's easier to work alone. It's easier for me to go into a room and write something than to deal with people.

■ ■ ■ ■

I think it's good for writers to be a little different, to maintain their allegiance to readers and not to activists or politicians, for whom they may have great, great sympathy. I just have to make my work as good as I can make it, make it as righteous as I can make it.

In one of the essays in *We Were Eight Years In Power,* I wrote, "Resistance is its own reward."[4] I think about the Black folk who have lived in this country all the years of their lives and never saw the end of slavery. Working in a field, knowing their children are going to be in that same field. Or Ida B. Wells who, in her time, was fighting for an anti-lynching bill — bill never gets passed.

And how do you think about the Panther Party? It sparks for a brief moment and captures the imagination of Black folk, who know all about the brutality this country inflicts on them through the police. But then the Party collapses and is pushed by the government into internecine fighting, to the point where Black folks are killing each other. How do we think about this? For me, this becomes a question of, "How do I want to live?" "What do I want my life to be about?"

Maybe this is my lack of a religious upbringing, but I get tremendous psychic reward — I would go so far as to say happiness — out of being on the side of those who are oppressed, as opposed to being on the side of the oppressor. I like where I am, but I enjoy the fight.

I enjoy the fight, you know what I mean?

I hope for victory, obviously, but when I wrote that piece about reparations, I had no notion that I would see reparations in my lifetime. Maybe not in anybody's lifetime. All this is about the fact of not accepting the lie — because most of racism and oppression is really some kind of dark lighting to get folks to accept the oppressor's rendition of history. For me, part of the reward is being able to say "NO.

No, this is *not* the world — it's oppression that is the lie."

We're made to accept that lie and to act as if it's not oppressive. Fighting that is probably the thing that motivates me the most.

We endure so many losses. How do we keep going? There are those folks who just go on, no matter what, but a lot of folks get despondent and sink into despair. But

289

here's what's important, no matter the result: If you stand up, in some profound way, you're already achieving something. The very act of standing up is an achievement. We need to remember that. It's not enough, of course. But it has meaning. I believe that.

My dad and Eddie sometimes talk about the movement "crazies." In political groups, both in civil rights and the Panthers, there are those people with bullhorns and the hyper-rhetoric. They have hardliner personalities most of us wouldn't want to deal with. They get joked about. But there's this tension. Those very folks are also, many times, the ones who are the movement's heartbeat, who are going to stay on it, who are the most consistent.

You know, I think it's sort of crazy to do this radical political thing in the first place. Put yourself outside the question of whether the Panther Party was right or not. Just ask yourself what it takes to be the sort of person to say, "I'm going to get some guns and head for the state capitol"? [*Laughs*]

Think of all the other priorities that anybody has to deal with on a day-in-day-out basis. And then to say, "OK, resistance is gonna be my life!" That's not a normal person. My dad ain't normal, you know what I mean? There's nothing normal about him.

In my first book, I wrote about my dad visiting his wife's bedside after she'd given birth to a new baby, his first son — and announcing to her that another woman he'd met in the Panthers was also about to give birth to his child.[5] I can understand people would judge him as sexist. But I think you have to see who he is from where he started. My dad had a father who was abusive toward him and toward the women in his life. It wasn't the family environment I would have my child in. My grandfather had children by my dad's mother and her two sisters, who were all much younger than he was. He was out of my dad's life by the time my dad was eight.

And at the time my dad was growing up in the 1950s and 1960s, there weren't a ton of models for how to conduct yourself as a just man. It's one thing to come up in this country as it is now, to have gone to a university with a women's studies department, to have been exposed to women in powerful positions. My dad didn't have that. I would never, never judge him free of sexism. But he was a good dude. He *is* a good,

good dude, and he is a just dude. Both of those things can be true at the same time.

You know my dad gave Eddie our old house? The house where I grew up, that's where Eddie lives now. That says something about the values I feel my dad and my mom were trying to inculcate in me when they started taking me to see Eddie all those years ago. That's also the task I take on when I write, the task of trying to see that Black people live as human beings.

My dad's friendship with Eddie is tremendous. And when my dad told me that Eddie was getting out of prison, I was ecstatic. I was really, really excited for him. 'Cause I have to be honest with you, I didn't think Eddie was ever going to get out.

Ta-Nehisi Coates, March 8, 2019

ACKNOWLEDGMENTS

This book has been a labor of love. So, to follow in Eddie's activist footsteps, I'd like to form a labor union. This union will be international, dedicated to some of the people who helped get this book together. Upfront, of course, are Eddie Conway and Paul Coates, whose wisdom, work, and spiritual beauty motivated this effort. This union also authorizes me finally to give credit to my partner in life and art, Laura Whitehorn, who forced me to delete several references to her throughout this book. Laura, here's something you can't edit: Without your passion and perspective and devotion, this book absolutely could not exist. Paul Coates was right in saying, "I got two for the price of one."

My karmic friendship with Randy Thomas also kept this project alive. Randy, your support allowed me to keep on this path —

293

especially after Trump got elected. So thank you.

Large appreciation goes to Leslie Thatcher, who, as my editor at *Truthout* in 2014, published my article about Eddie's release and an interview that helped start this project.

Many thanks to Dan Berger, for his help, his encouragement, his writings, his enviable knowledge of the Panthers, and so much more.

Deep gratitude to Martin Paddio, my supervisor at Monthly Review Press, where he cut me so much slack for so long. To Michael Yates, MR editor, for his interest and support. To Martha Cameron, for her smart feedback. And I thank Paul Schindler, my editor at *Gay City News,* who let me skip so many deadlines. By some miracle, I apparently still write for *GCN.*

Unsolicited thanks keep pouring into union coffers; specifically, to Bob Boyle, Eddie's attorney, who's been there year after year for Eddie and for so many others inside; Dominque Stevenson, for being so smart and always on it, and for her formidable spirit; Elizabeth Terhune and Mark Sullivan, for their devoted years of the cat-sitting that allowed all those trips to Baltimore; Lumumba Bandele for his activism and inside info; Diane Samuels, for being a dedicated writer and consummate friend; Valentina DuBasky, exemplary artist, who encouraged me to stand up; Tynan Jarrett, my pal, for being there every year in this years-long endeavor; Leila Pourtavaf, for her intellect, passion, and compassion; Herman Bell, a *former* political prisoner, for finally getting the fuck out of prison and letting me get back to this book; Ellen Sklar, for being an ace-encourager, friend, and Moriarty to my Sherlock; Tim Murphy, writer and activist, whose example continues to encourage and inspire; to Linda Jones Scott, for that Big Picture perspective; Barbara Zeller, for asking me every time we got together, *"How's it going?"* and then listening to my answer; David Gilbert, for calling from prison, asking that same question, and also listening; Treva Ellison and Freda Fair, for offering knowledge and wise perspectives on teaching Panther history to today's students; Maya Schenwar, for her years of friendship, support, writing, editing, and that magical suggestion that I contact Haymarket Books. Additional thanks to Paul Coates, this time for his help with final edits. General thanks to Laura's excellent sister, Marion Minton, and mine, Nancy.

Finally, to the people at Haymarket Books,

notably Julie Fain, Ashley Smith, Rory Fanning, and Maya Marshall, I thank you for your vision, focus, dedication, support, and patience.

THE BLACK PANTHER PARTY TEN POINT PROGRAM

What you are about to read is probably the earliest version of the Panthers' Ten Point Program, which was published, fully capitalized, in the May 15, 1967, edition of the Black Panther *newspaper.*

WHAT WE WANT NOW! WHAT WE BELIEVE

TO THOSE POOR SOULS WHO DON'T KNOW BLACK HISTORY, THE BELIEFS AND DESIRES OF THE BLACK PANTHER PARTY FOR SELF DEFENSE MAY SEEM UNREASONABLE. TO BLACK PEOPLE, THE TEN POINTS COVERED ARE ABSOLUTELY ESSENTIAL TO SURVIVAL. WE HAVE LISTENED TO THE RIOT PRODUCING WORDS "THESE THINGS TAKE TIME" FOR 400 YEARS. THE BLACK PANTHER PARTY KNOWS WHAT BLACK PEOPLE WANT AND NEED. BLACK

UNITY AND SELF DEFENSE WILL MAKE THESE DEMANDS A REALITY.

WHAT WE WANT

1. WE WANT FREEDOM. WE WANT POWER TO DETERMINE THE DESTINY OF OUR BLACK COMMUNITY.

2. WE WANT FULL EMPLOYMENT FOR OUR PEOPLE.

3. WE WANT AN END TO THE ROBBERY BY THE WHITE MAN OF OUR BLACK COMMUNITY.

4. WE WANT DECENT HOUSING, FIT FOR SHELTER [OF] HUMAN BEINGS.

5. WE WANT EDUCATION FOR OUR PEOPLE THAT EXPOSES THE TRUE NATURE OF THIS DECADENT AMERICAN SOCIETY. WE WANT EDUCATION THAT TEACHES US OUR TRUE HISTORY AND OUR ROLE IN THE PRESENT-DAY SOCIETY.

6. WE WANT ALL BLACK MEN TO BE EXEMPT FROM MILITARY SERVICE.

7. WE WANT AN IMMEDIATE END TO

POLICE BRUTALITY AND MURDER OF BLACK PEOPLE.

8. WE WANT FREEDOM FOR ALL BLACK MEN HELD IN FEDERAL, STATE, COUNTY, AND CITY PRISONS AND JAILS.

9. WE WANT ALL BLACK PEOPLE WHEN BROUGHT TO TRIAL TO BE TRIED IN COURT BY A JURY OF THEIR PEER GROUP OR PEOPLE FROM THEIR BLACK COMMUNITIES. AS DEFINED BY THE CONSTITUTION OF THE UNITED STATES.

10. WE WANT LAND, BREAD, HOUSING, EDUCATION, CLOTHING, JUSTICE AND PEACE.

(As far as I can tell, edits to later versions of the Program are relatively minor. However, two changes are worth noting:
1) the much-discussed "Plebiscite" was added to point ten in the October 1968 edition of the Black Panther, *just after a Panther delegation had gone to the UN: a "United Nations-supervised plebiscite to be held throughout the black colony in which only black colonial subjects will be allowed to*

participate for the purpose of determining the will of black people as to their national destiny"; and

2) "white man" in point three was replaced by "capitalist" — probably on the suggestion of Fred Hampton.[1] The following section, "What We Believe," was interspersed among the Ten Points in later versions.)

WHAT WE BELIEVE

1. WE BELIEVE THAT BLACK PEOPLE WILL NOT BE FREE UNTIL WE ARE ABLE TO DETERMINE OUR DESTINY.

2. WE BELIEVE THAT THE FEDERAL GOVERNMENT IS RESPONSIBLE AND OBLIGATED TO GIVE EVERY MAN EMPLOYMENT OR A GUARANTEED INCOME. WE BELIEVE THAT IF THE WHITE AMERICAN BUSINESS MEN WILL NOT GIVE FULL EMPLOYMENT, THEN THE MEANS OF PRODUCTION SHOULD BE TAKEN FROM THE BUSINESS MEN AND PLACED IN THE COMMUNITY SO THAT THE PEOPLE OF THE COMMUNITY CAN ORGANIZE AND EMPLOY ALL OF ITS PEOPLE AND GIVE A HIGH STANDARD OF LIVING.

3. WE BELIEVE THAT THIS RACIST

GOVERNMENT HAS ROBBED US AND NOW WE ARE DEMANDING THE OVERDUE DEBT OF FORTY ACRES AND TWO MULES. FORTY ACRES AND TWO MULES WAS PROMISED 100 YEARS AGO AS RETRIBUTION FOR SLAVE LABOR AND MASS MURDER OF BLACK PEOPLE. WE WILL ACCEPT THE PAYMENT IN CURRENCY WHICH WILL BE DISTRIBUTED TO OUR MANY COMMUNITIES: THE GERMANS ARE NOW AIDING THE JEWS IN ISRAEL FOR THE GENOCIDE OF THE JEWISH PEOPLE. THE GERMANS MURDERED 6,000,000 JEWS. THE AMERICAN RACIST HAS TAKEN PART IN THE SLAUGHTER OF OVER 50,000,000 BLACK PEOPLE; THEREFORE, WE FEEL THAT THIS IS A MODEST DEMAND THAT WE MAKE.

4. WE BELIEVE THAT IF THE WHITE LANDLORDS WILL NOT GIVE DECENT HOUSING TO OUR BLACK COMMUNITY, THEN THE HOUSING AND THE LAND SHOULD BE MADE INTO COOPERATIVES SO THAT OUR COMMUNITY, WITH GOVERNMENT AID, CAN BUILD AND MAKE DE-

CENT HOUSING FOR ITS PEOPLE.

5. WE BELIEVE IN AN EDUCATIONAL SYSTEM THAT WILL GIVE TO OUR PEOPLE A KNOWLEDGE OF SELF. IF A MAN DOES NOT HAVE KNOWLEDGE OF HIMSELF AND HIS POSITION IN SOCIETY AND THE WORLD, THEN HE HAS LITTLE CHANCE TO RELATE TO ANYTHING ELSE.

6. WE BELIEVE THAT BLACK PEOPLE SHOULD NOT BE FORCED TO FIGHT IN THE MILITARY SERVICE TO DEFEND A RACIST GOVERNMENT THAT DOES NOT PROTECT US. WE WILL NOT FIGHT AND KILL OTHER PEOPLE OF COLOR IN THE WORLD WHO, LIKE BLACK PEOPLE, ARE BEING VICTIMIZED BY THE WHITE RACIST GOVERNMENT OF AMERICA. WE WILL PROTECT OURSELVES FROM THE FORCE AND VIOLENCE OF THE RACIST POLICE AND THE RACIST MILITARY, BY WHATEVER MEANS NECESSARY.

7. WE BELIEVE WE CAN END POLICE BRUTALITY IN OUR BLACK COMMUNITY BY ORGANIZING BLACK SELF DEFENSE GROUPS THAT ARE

DEDICATED TO DEFENDING OUR BLACK COMMUNITY FROM RACIST POLICE OPPRESSION AND BRUTALITY. THE SECOND AMENDMENT OF THE CONSTITUTION OF THE UNITED STATES GIVES US A RIGHT TO BEAR ARMS. WE THEREFORE BELIEVE THAT ALL BLACK PEOPLE SHOULD ARM THEMSELVES FOR SELF DEFENSE.

8. WE BELIEVE THAT ALL BLACK PEOPLE SHOULD BE RELEASED FROM THE MANY JAILS AND PRISONS BECAUSE THEY HAVE NOT RECEIVED A FAIR AND IMPARTIAL TRIAL.

9. WE BELIEVE THAT THE COURTS SHOULD FOLLOW THE UNITED STATES CONSTITUTION SO THAT BLACK PEOPLE WILL RECEIVE FAIR TRIALS. THE 14TH AMENDMENT OF THE US CONSTITUTION GIVES A MAN A RIGHT TO BE TRIED BY HIS PEER GROUP. A PEER IS A PERSON FROM A SIMILAR ECONOMIC, SOCIAL, RELIGIOUS, GEOGRAPHICAL, ENVIRONMENTAL, HISTORICAL AND RACIAL BACKGROUND. TO DO THIS THE COURT WILL BE FORCED

TO SELECT A JURY FROM THE BLACK COMMUNITY FROM WHICH THE BLACK DEFENDANT CAME. WE HAVE BEEN, AND ARE BEING TRIED BY ALL WHITE JURIES THAT HAVE NO UNDERSTANDING OF THE "AVERAGE REASONING MAN" OF THE BLACK COMMUNITY.

10. WHEN IN THE COURSE OF HUMAN EVENTS, IT BECOMES NECESSARY FOR ONE PEOPLE TO DISSOLVE THE POLITICAL BONDS WHICH HAVE CONNECTED THEM WITH ANOTHER, AND TO ASSUME AMONG THE POWERS OF THE EARTH, THE SEPARATE AND EQUAL STATION TO WHICH THE LAWS OF NATURE AND NATURE'S GOD ENTITLE THEM, A DECENT RESPECT TO THE OPINIONS OF MANKIND REQUIRES THAT THEY SHOULD DECLARE THE CAUSES WHICH IMPEL THEM TO SEPARATION. WE HOLD THESE TRUTHS TO BE SELF-EVIDENT, THAT ALL MEN ARE CREATED EQUAL, THAT THEY ARE ENDOWED BY THEIR CREATOR WITH CERTAIN INALIENABLE RIGHTS, THAT AMONG THESE ARE LIFE, LIBERTY AND THE

PURSUIT OF HAPPINESS. THAT TO SECURE THESE RIGHTS, GOVERN- MENTS ARE INSTITUTED AMONG MEN, DERIVING THEIR JUST POW- ERS FROM THE CONSENT OF THE GOVERNED, THAT WHENEVER ANY FORM OF GOVERNMENT BECOMES DESTRUCTIVE OF THESE ENDS, IT IS THE RIGHT OF PEOPLE TO ALTER OR TO ABOLISH IT, AND TO INSTI- TUTE NEW GOVERNMENT, LAYING ITS FOUNDATION ON SUCH PRINCI- PLES AND ORGANIZING ITS POWERS IN SUCH FORM AS TO THEM SHALL SEEM MOST LIKELY TO EFFECT THEIR SAFETY AND HAPPINESS. PRUDENCE, INDEED, WILL DICTATE THAT GOVERNMENTS LONG ESTAB- LISHED SHOULD NOT BE CHANGED FOR LIGHT AND TRANSIENT CAUSES; AND ACCORDINGLY ALL EXPERIENCE HATH SHEWN, THAT MANKIND ARE MORE DISPOSED TO SUFFER, WHILE EVILS ARE SUFFER- ABLE, THAN TO RIGHT THEMSELVES BY ABOLISHING THE FORMS TO WHICH THEY ARE ACCUSTOMED. BUT WHEN A LONG TRAIN OF ABUSES AND USURPATIONS, PURSU- ING INVARIABLY THE SAME OBJECT,

EVINCES A DESIGN TO REDUCE THEM UNDER ABSOLUTE DESPOTISM, IT IS THEIR RIGHT, IT IS THEIR DUTY, TO THROW OFF SUCH GOVERNMENT, AND TO PROVIDE NEW GUARDS FOR THEIR FUTURE SECURITY.

GLOSSARY

Ahidiana-Habari: African American publisher, now defunct, of mostly poetry, essays, and novels, based in New Orleans, and one of Paul Coates's early influences in starting Black Classic Press. An example of its books is *Kalamu ya Salaam, Revolutionary Love: Poems and Essays,* 1978.

Yosef Alfredo Antonio Ben-Jochannan: (1918–2015) US historian, Afrocentric scholar, and author of such books as *Africa: Mother of Western Civilization* (Baltimore: Black Classic Press, 1997). "Dr. Ben," as he was called, was often published by Black Classic Press.

The Black Panther: official newspaper of the BPP. Started by the Oakland chapter in 1967, it soon spread nationally, then internationally. From 1968 to 1971 it was rated the most popular Black newspaper in the United States, selling over 300,000 copies every week, at 25 cents per copy.

See, e.g., "Remembering the Black Panther Party Newspaper, The True Voice of the People, April 25, 1967–September 1980," California Historical Society: https://summerof.love/remembering-the -black-panther-party-newspaper/ and various websites and interviews with ex-Panther and archivist, Billy X Jennings.

Bogle-L'Ouverture Publications (BLP): London-based publisher founded in 1968 by Guyanese activists. It was the first publisher of *How Europe Underdeveloped Africa* by Walter Rodney in 1972. The press was a guiding presence for Paul Coates as he started Black Classic Press.

Elaine Brown: (b. 1943) Oakland-based Chairwoman of the Black Panther Party, 1974–77. See *A Taste of Power: A Black Woman's Story* (New York: Anchor Books, 1993).

H. Rap Brown: (b. 1943) chair of the Student Nonviolent Organizing Committee and later Panther Party Minister of Justice. He converted to Islam in prison during the 1970s, and became Jamil Abdullah Al-Amin. He is currently serving a life sentence, for allegedly killing a police officer in 2000. See, e.g., Arun Kundnani, "Rethinking H. Rap Brown and Black Power," *Black Perspectives,* Sept. 29, 2018, site:

https://www.aaihs.org/rethinking-h-rap
-brown-and-black-power/.

Penelope L. Bullock: (1922–2010) African American historian and mentor to Paul Coates. She wrote *The Afro-American Periodical Press, 1838–1909* (Baton Rouge: Louisiana State University Press, 1981), a study of publications often overlooked in the analysis of the Black press.

Stokely Carmichael: (1941–1998) born in Trinidad, Carmichael became an activist while attending Howard University and was one of the original Freedom Riders of the Student Nonviolent Coordinating Committee. Inspired by Malcolm X, he helped develop the "Black power" theory, and joined the Black Panther Party, then later joined the All-African People's Revolutionary Party. Fleeing COINTELPRO, he lived in Africa for several years and chose the name Kwame Ture. The CIA document Eddie refers to in "I Was One of the People They Rolled Up," was evidently planted by the FBI.

Church Committee: in 1975, the US Senate Select Committee to Study Governmental Operations with Respect to Intelligence Activities (Church Committee) investigated intelligence/surveillance abuses by the FBI, CIA, and NSA. Chaired by Idaho

Senator Frank Church, the investigation released its findings in 1976 to reveal the existence of the FBI's COINTELPRO. See US Senate site: https://www.intel ligence.senate.gov/resources/intelligence -related-commissions.

Coalition of Friends: another name for the Tubman House in Baltimore, a community project that Eddie helped start about two months after his release from prison in 2014. Site: https://www .tubmanhousebaltimore.org.

COINTELPRO: "Counterintelligence Program" devised by the Federal Bureau of Investigation. Beginning in 1956, COINTELPRO came into its own during the 1960s through mid-1970s, in its largely successful efforts to "neutralize" various liberation and antiwar groups, viewed as anti-American. It's important to know, however, that the FBI did not infiltrate, monitor, and destroy movements alone; it often worked in conjunction with other government intelligence agencies and with local police forces. It's also recognized that surveillance technology and legal authority were, during COINTELPRO's reign, in relatively early development.

Afeni Shakur Davis: (1947–2016) former Black Panther, who, as a defendant in the

Panther 21 case, spent two years in jail, and gave birth to a son, Lesane Parish Crooks, later renamed Tupac, a few weeks after her release. In 1975, she married Mutulu Shakur, the father of their daughter, Sekyiwa.

Elinor Des Verney Sinnette: (1925–2020) a great inspiration to Paul Coates in scholarship and publishing, she wrote *Arthur Alfonso Schomburg: Black Bibliophile & Collector: A Biography* (Wayne, IN: Wayne State University Press, 1989). With Thomas C. Battle, Sinnette and Coates edited *Black Bibliophiles and Collectors: Preservers of Black History* (Howard University Press, 1990).

The East: a community education and arts organization founded in Brooklyn, New York, in 1969 by African American activists focused on self-determination and Black consciousness. It produced a biweekly national news publication, and hosted performers, including some of the Last Poets. See Kwasi Konadu, *A View from the East: Black Cultural Nationalism and Education in New York City,* 2nd edition (Syracuse, NY: Syracuse University Press, 2009).

Dr. Charles Finch III: little-known historian and Egyptian scholar. Author of many books, among them *Echoes of the Old Darkland: Themes from the African Eden* (Location unknown: Khenti, 1991).

Friend of a Friend: sponsored by the American Friends Service Committee, Friend of a Friend works in Maryland prisons to educate and mentor people in conflict resolution. The program was started by Eddie Conway and Dominque Stevenson in the early 2000s. See AFSC site: https://www.afsc.org/program/friend-friend-program.

George Jackson Prison Movement: organized in Baltimore in the early 1970s by Paul Coates and Eddie Conway to help connect people in prisons with the outside world, largely in the form of Black literature and culture. An FBI memo dated December 26, 1972, says that the Baltimore office failed to find any extremist activity, but "will continue to follow the activities of the George Jackson Prison Movement." See https://archive.org/details/GeorgeJacksonPrisonMovement/page/n1.

Freddie Gray: (1989–2015) a twenty-five-year-old Black man, arrested on April 12, 2015, by Baltimore police who alleged that Gray possessed an illegal knife. After being thrown inside a police van, Gray suffered massive spinal cord injuries, fell into a coma, and died on April 19. His injuries were almost certainly due to a police "rough ride," an illegal but fairly common practice in which suspects are handcuffed, placed in police wagons, and driven violently around, to incur as much physical damage as possible, thus sparing police from being accused of actually beating people in custody. Gray's death prompted months of outrage and public protest.

Gulf of Tonkin Incident: on August 2, 1964, two US naval destroyers engaged militarily with North Vietnamese boats. Although little or no damage resulted, the incident and the manipulated military intelligence that ensued led to the Gulf of Tonkin resolution, which gave President Johnson the authority to take any measures necessary to promote "peace and security" in the region. It effectively started the Vietnam War.

Fred Hampton: (1948–1969) Chairman of the Illinois Panther Party and Deputy Chairman of the National BPP, Hampton, by all accounts, was a gifted activist and upstanding human being, whose popularity across racial communities attracted the scrutiny of COINTELPRO. Hampton, with BPP member Mark Clark, was assassinated by Chicago police on December 4, 1969.

Drusilla Dunjee Houston: (1876–1941) educator and independent historian, whose brother, Roscoe, founded the *Oklahoma Black Dispatch,* the first Black newspaper in Oklahoma City. Houston wrote for the paper, but her most memorable achievement is her book, *Wonderful Ethiopians of the Ancient Cushite Empire* (Baltimore: Black Classic Press, 2013).

George Jackson: (1941–1971) sentenced at age eighteen to one year to life for stealing seventy dollars from a gas station, Jackson became a revolutionary activist and author inside San Quentin Prison. His book, *Soledad Brother: The Prison Letters of George Jackson,* galvanized the prison activist movement in 1970. *Blood in My Eye,* his second book, was completed only days before Jackson was killed by corrections officers during an alleged escape attempt.

Jihad Press: started by LeRoi Jones (later Amiri Baraka), who used the press to publish his own poetry and plays, e.g., *Slave Ship: An Historical Pageant* (Newark, NJ: Jihad Publications, 1966). Jihad was another publishing inspiration for Paul Coates in starting Black Classic Press.

Alain Locke: (1885–1954) writer, educator, first African American Rhodes scholar. A recent biography is *The New Negro: The Life of Alain Locke,* Jeffrey C. Stewart (Oxford University Press, 2018).

Haki R. Madhubuti: (b. 1942) originally Don L. Lee, Madhubuti is an author, poet, publisher, and colleague of Paul Coates. See, e.g., *Liberation Narratives: New and Collected Poems: 1966–2009,* among many other books. In 1967 he started the Third World Press. It remains one of the largest and most successful Black-owned presses in the United States.

Maryland Penitentiary Inter-Communal Survival Collective: a committee for prison clean-up and prisoners' rights, started by Eddie Conway, among others, shortly after Eddie began his sentence in 1971. See Eddie's mention, "I Didn't Want to See a Dude" in Chapter 10, "Life Plus Thirty Years"; also, Eddie's accounts in his book, *Marshall Law: The Life & Times of a Baltimore Black Panther* (Oakland, CA: AK Press, 2011).

National Committee to Combat Fascism: began in 1969 following the BPP-sponsored United Front Against Fascism Conference. It later became the Intercom-munal Committee to Combat Fascism.

The Berkeley Chapter was unique in that it was comprised mostly of white people who represented the local Panther chapter. See "It's About Time: Black Panther Party Legacy and Alumni": http://www.itsabout timebpp.com/Our_Stories/Chapter1/The _iccf.html. The Louisiana chapter, started by Malik Rahim, later became a BPP chapter. See Orissa Arend, *Showdown in Desire: The Black Panthers Take a Stand in New Orleans* (Fayetteville: University of Arkansas Press, 2010).

New Beacon Books: an early literary model for Paul Coates, this London-based publishing house was founded in 1966 to specialize in Black British, Caribbean, African, African American, and Asian literature. It was the first UK publisher of Caribbean literature, and exists today.

Newark rebellion or Newark riot: began in Newark, New Jersey, on July 12, 1967, when police arrested an African American cab driver, purportedly for traffic violations and physical assault. Members of the Congress for Racial Equality (CORE), visiting the cab driver at the precinct, demanded he be hospitalized, due to injuries sustained during his arrest. Word spread throughout a community already tired of police harassment and racial discrimination. Ensuing uproar motivated New Jersey Mayor Hugh Addonizio to call in the National Guard. By the time it ended, on July 17, the rebellion resulted in the deaths of some twenty-six people, mostly African American. Approximately 750 were injured, over one thousand were jailed, and property damage topped $10 million.

Panther 21: in April 1969, twenty-one members of the New York City Black Panther Party were indicted on charges of conspiring to bomb five department stores, a police station, railroad tracks, the Bronx Botanical Gardens, and other municipal targets. Held for two years without bail, the defendants were eventually acquitted, after forty-five minutes of jury deliberation. See Albert Woodfox's account of meeting the detained Panthers as a prisoner himself in the New York City Tombs, *Solitary: My Story of Transformation and Hope* (Grove Press, 2019). Also see Murray Kempton, *The Briar Patch: The Trial of the Panther 21* (New York: Da Capo Press, 1997).

Leonard Peltier: a citizen of the Anishinaabe and Lakota Nations and member of the American Indian Movement (AIM), Peltier has been in prison since 1976, convicted of the shooting deaths of two FBI agents on the Pine Ridge Reservation in South Dakota.

Plebiscite: contained in the revised tenth point of the BPP's Ten Point Program: "We want land, bread, housing, education, clothing, justice and peace. And as our major political objective, a United Nations–supervised plebiscite to be held throughout the Black colony in which only Black colonial subjects will be allowed to participate for the purpose of determining the will of Black people as to their national destiny." Probably added to the original Ten Point Program in October 1968, after a Panther delegation was sent to the United Nations. (See *Black Against Empire,* Bloom and Martin, chapter 3, footnote 8.)

Republic of New Africa (RNA): Black nationalist organization founded in 1968 Detroit, one year after the Detroit Rebellion. Premised on self-de-termination, with the goal of creating an independent Black republic from the Southern states of South Carolina, Georgia, Alabama, Mississippi, and Louisiana, the Provisional Government of the Republic of New Afrika (spelling changed) exists today.

Arturo Alfonso Schomburg: (1874–1938)

Puerto Rican author, activist, and historian, for whom the Schomburg Center for Research in Black Culture in New York City is named.

Student Nonviolent Coordinating Committee (SNCC): founded in 1960 as an interracial, nonviolent group, pivotal in the growth of the civil rights movement. SNCC became more militant as the 1960s progressed, calling for Black Power with leaders such as Stokely Carmichael (later, Kwame Ture) and H. Rap Brown (later, Jamil Abdullah Al-Amin). SNCC was often allied with the BPP.

Ten Point Program: guidelines for the Black Panther Party of Self-Defense set out by Bobby Seale, Huey Newton, and other Panthers as bedrock goals and ideals for self-determination. It was altered slightly from the earliest version, which was published, fully capitalized, in the May 15, 1967, edition of the *Black Panther* newspaper. Later versions in the paper and elsewhere are, ironically, dated October 1966.

Unger Decision/Unger v. Maryland: the legal precedent that gave Eddie Conway his freedom. In order to comply with due process as stated in the US Constitution, juries must be convinced beyond a reasonable doubt that someone charged with a crime is guilty before that jury can convict a defendant. However, for years, Maryland judges were required to instruct juries that they were to decide cases as judges of the facts and the law, and that legal advice from a judge, such as "innocent until proven guilty" or "proof beyond a reasonable doubt" did not have to be followed in rendering a verdict. This practice was stopped in 1980, but the Unger decision in 2012 was momentous in that it applied retroactively to people convicted before 1980. See Robert Siegel, "From a Life Term to Life on the Outside: When Aging Felons Are Freed," NPR, *All Things Considered,* February 18, 2016, site: https://www.npr.org/2016/02/18/467057 603/from-a-life-term-to-life-on-the -outside-when-aging-felons-are-freed; also "The Ungers, Five Years and Counting: A Case Study in Safely Reducing Long Prison Terms and Saving Taxpayer Dollars," Justice Policy Institute, January 2019, site: http://www.justicepolicy.org/ research/12320.

David Walker: (1796–1830) African American journalist and anti-slavery activist, who wrote the groundbreaking "David Walker's Appeal: To the Colored Citizens of the World, but in Particular, and Very Expressly, to those of the United States of America." Originally published in 1830, the Black Classic Press currently publishes it.

Writers and Readers Publishing Co-operative: a publishing contemporary of Paul Coates, it began in London, in 1974, but later became For Beginners LLC, and is now based in Danbury, Connecticut. It has published a popular series of nonfiction graphic books documenting political and scientific topics, including *Marx for Beginners, Freud for Beginners,* and *Darwin for Beginners.*

SELECTED BIBLIOGRAPHY

A complete list of books, films, and websites about the Black Panther Party and the historical context from which it arose would probably fill volumes. For the purposes of this book, I'm only listing a few of the sources that have helped me to understand the immensity of the history and humanity that have made up the Panther Party and the lives of Eddie Conway and Paul Coates. Just know there is so much more out there.

Books

Mumia Abu-Jamal, *We Want Freedom: A Life in the Black Panther Party* (Cambridge, MA: South End Press, 2004)

Dan Berger, *Captive Nation: Black Prison Organizing in the Civil Rights Era* (Chapel Hill: University of North Carolina Press, 2014)

Dhoruba Bin Wahad, Jamal Joseph, Sekou

Odinga, déqui kioni-sadiki, Matt Meyer, Mumia Abu-Jamal, and Imam Jamil Al-Amin, *Look for Me in the Whirlwind: From the Panther 21 to 21st-Century Revolutions* (Oakland, CA: PM Press, 2017)

Joshua Bloom and Waldo E. Martin, Jr., *Black Against Empire: The History and Politics of the Black Panther Party* (Berkeley: University of California Press, 2013)

Safiya Bukhari, *The War Before: The True Life Story of Becoming a Black Panther, Keeping the Faith in Prison, & Fighting for Those Left Behind*, Laura Whitehorn, ed. (New York: Feminist Press, 2010)

Emory Douglas, *Black Panther: The Revolutionary Art of Emory Douglas* (New York: Rizzoli, 2007)

Stokely Carmichael (Kwame Ture) with Ekueme Michael Thelwell, *Ready for Revolution: The Life and Struggles of Stokely Carmichael* (New York: Scribner, 2003)

Ta-Nehisi Coates, *The Beautiful Struggle: A Father, Two Sons, and an Unlikely Road to Manhood* (New York: Spiegel & Grau, 2009)

Ta-Nehisi Coates, *Between the World and Me* (New York: Spiegel and Grau, 2015)

Ta-Nehisi Coates, *We Were Eight Years in*

Power: An American Tragedy (New York: One World, 2017)

Marshall "Eddie" Conway and Dominque Stevenson, *Marshall Law: The Life & Times of a Baltimore Black Panther* (Oakland, CA: AK Press, 2011)

Don Cox, *Just Another Nigger: My Life in the Black Panther Party* (Berkeley, CA: Heyday, 2019)

Angela Davis, *Angela Davis: An Autobiography* (New York: International Publishers Co., 1988)

W. E. B. DuBois, *We Charge Genocide: The Historic Petition to the United Nations for Relief from a Crime of the United States Government Against the Negro People* (New York: Civil Rights Congress, 1st ed., 1951). Online.

Frantz Fanon, *The Wretched of the Earth* (New York: Grove, 2005)

Jeffrey Haas, *The Assassination of Fred Hampton: How the FBI and the Chicago Police Murdered a Black Panther* (Chicago: Chicago Review Press, 2011)

Alex Haley, *The Autobiography of Malcolm X: As Told to Alex Haley* (New York: Ballantine Books, 1992)

Drusilla Dunjee Houston, *Wonderful Ethiopians of the Ancient Cushite Empire* (Baltimore: Black Classic Press, 2013)

George Jackson, *Soledad Brother: The Prison Letters of George Jackson* (New York: Bantam, 1970)

Joy James, *Warfare in the American Homeland: Policing and Prison in a Penal Democracy* (Durham, NC: Duke University Press, 2007)

Charles E. Jones, ed., *The Black Panther Party Reconsidered* (Baltimore: Black Classic Press, 1998). See especially, Winston A. Grady-Willis, "The Black Panther Party: State Repression and Political Prisoners."

Robin D. G. Kelley, *Freedom Dreams: The Black Radical Imagination* (Boston: Beacon Press, 2002)

Murray Kempton, *The Briar Patch: The Trial of the Panther 21* (New York: Da Capo Press, 1997)

Reginald Major, *A Panther Is a Black Cat* (Baltimore: Black Classic Press, 2006)

Elaine Mokhtefi, *Algiers, Third World Capital: Freedom Fighters, Revolutionaries, Black Panthers* (Brooklyn, NY: Verso Books, 2018)

Leonard Peltier, *Prison Writings: My Life Is My Sun Dance* (New York: St. Martin's Griffin, 2000)

Barbara Ransby, *Making All Black Lives Matter* (Oakland, CA: University of California Press, 2018)

Assata Shakur, *Assata: An Autobiography* (New York: Lawrence Hill Books, 2001)

Robyn Spencer, *The Revolution Has Come: Black Power, Gender, and the Black Panther Party in Oakland* (Durham, NC: Duke University Press, 2016)

David Walker, *David Walker's Appeal: To the Colored Citizens of the World, but in Particular, and Very Expressly, to Those of the United States of America* (Baltimore: Black Classic Press, 1997)

Yohuru Williams, *Black Politics/White Power: Civil Rights, Black Power, and the Black Panthers in New Haven* (Hoboken, NJ: Wiley-Blackwell, 2000)

Albert Woodfox, *Solitary: My Story of Transformation and Hope* (New York: Grove Press, 2019)

Malcolm X, *By Any Means Necessary* (Malcolm X Speeches and Writings) (New York: Pathfinder Press, 1992)

Films, TV

All Power to the People, Lee Lew Lee, 1996; Lee, a former Panther, documents political history of the BPP

American Revolution 2, Mike Gray/Howard Alk, 1969; documentary on the 1968 Democratic National Convention and radical aftermath

Baltimore Rising, HBO documentary on the killing of Freddie Gray, 2017

The Battle of Algiers, Gillo Pontecorvo, 1967

The Black Panthers: Vanguard of the Revolution, Stanley Nelson, 2015; probably best-known Panther documentary, where you can see almost eleven seconds of Paul Coates

The Black Power Mixtape 1967–1975, Göran Olsson, 2011; documentary look at originals of the US Black Power Movement, taken from footage shot by Swedish filmmakers in the 1960s and '70s

COINTELPRO 101, Claude Marks, documentary film, 2010

Eyes on the Prize, Blackside, PBS documentary series on the civil rights movement, first aired 1987

The FBI's War on Black America, Deb Ellis, Denis Mueller, 1990

Finding Your Roots, Henry Louis Gates; "Author Ta-Nehisi Coates, activist Janet Mock and filmmaker Ava DuVernay, learn new details about their ancestors," PBS, October 24, 2017

Free Angela and All Political Prisoners, Shola

Lynch, 2012

Freedom Riders, Stanley Nelson, 2011; documentary chronicling the civil rights movement's freedom rides against racial segregation

Ghosts of Attica, Brad Lichtenstein, 2001; one of a few documentaries on the 1971 rebellion at Attica Prison, NY

Hearts and Minds, Peter Davis, 1974; made during the Vietnam War, the film intersperses interviews of US military leaders with scenes of GI violence and cruelty

A Huey P. Newton Story, Roger Guenveur Smith, 2001; film of Smith's one-person show on Newton

The Murder of Fred Hampton, Howard Alk, Mike Gray, 1971; begun as a documentary of Hampton; Hampton's murder became the focus of this film

Panther, Mario Van Peebles, 1995; based on Van Peebles's novel

Spies of Mississippi, Dawn Porter, 2014

"Tour of Black Classic Press," Paul Coates with host Peter Slen, CSPAN, February 20, 2018, site: https://www.c-span.org/video/?441322-2/tour-black-classic-press. Paul Coates has appeared on other CSPAN segments.

Internet

Baltimore Afro American Newspaper Archives, 1912–1978: https://newspaperarchive .com/us/md/baltimore/baltimore-afro -american/

It's About Time: a website of Panther records and events: http://www.itsabouttimebpp .com/INDEX_PHOTOGALLERY.HTML

Sitemap: http://www.itsabouttimebpp.com/ home/sitemap_index.html

For a Partial Archive of the *Black Panther* Paper:

http://itsabouttimebpp.com/BPP _Newspapers/bpp_newspapers_index.html

Freedom Archives: https://freedomarchives .org

Specifically for *Panther News Service* documents:

https://search.freedomarchives.org/ search .php?view_collection=90

Black Classic Press: http://www .blackclassicbooks.com

The Real News Network: https:// therealnews.com

Emory Douglas: https://www.aiga.org/ design-journeys-emory-douglas

Leonard Peltier support: https://www

.whoisleonardpeltier.info

Websites for Former Members of the Black Panther Party, Still Incarcerated:

Many of these people have had websites constructed by outside supporters.

For those without individual websites, a basic resource site is *The Jericho*

National Movement: https://www.thejericho movement.com/

Mumia Abu-Jamal: https://www.prisonradio .org/media/audio/mumia

Sundiata Acoli: http://www.sundiataacoli.org

Jamil Al-Amin: no website; Jericho: https:// www.thejerichomovement.com/profile/al -amin-jamil-abdullah

Veronza Bowers: http://www.veronza.org

Romaine 'Chip' Fitzgerald, no website; Jericho: https://www.thejerichomovement .com/profile/fitzgerald-romaine-chip

Ruchell 'Cinque' Magee, no website; Jericho: https://www.thejerichomovement.com/ profile/magee-ruchell-cinque

Jalil Muntaqim: https://freejalil.com

Ed Poindexter: no website; Jericho: https:// www.thejerichomovement.com/profile/ poindexter-ed

Kamau Sadik: http://freekamau.com

Dr. Mutulu Shakur: http://mutulushakur

.com/site/

Russell Maroon Shoatz: https://russell maroonshoats.wordpress.com

NOTES

Preface: Life, Politics, The Revolution

1. Joshua Bloom and Waldo Martin, *Black Against Empire: The History and Politics of the Black Panther Party* (University of California Press, 2013), 40. "[O]nce there was little legal segregation left to defy, the insurgent Civil Rights Movement fell apart."

Chapter 2: Marshall Edward Conway — Look, They Got Our Stuff

1. Freddie Gray: twenty-five-year-old Black man, arrested on April 12, 2015, by Baltimore police who alleged Gray possessed an illegal knife. Shortly after being thrown into a police van, Gray fell into a coma and died on April 19. His death, attributed to spinal cord injuries inflicted by police, prompted weeks of outrage and

public protest.

Chapter 4: Eddie Conway: How the Army Happened

1. For a glimpse into the reality of African Americans fighting in the Vietnam War, see Wallace Terry's *Bloods, Black Veterans of the Vietnam War: An Oral History* (New York: Presidio Press, 1984).

Chapter 7: They Used Our People to Kill Our People

1. Michael X. Delli Carpini, "Black Panther Party: 1966-1982," in *The Encyclopedia of Third Parties in America,* I. Ness & J. Ciment, eds. (Armonk, NY: Sharpe Reference, 2000), *190–97* https://repository.upenn.edu/cgi/viewcontent.cgi?article=1004&context=asc_papers.
2. This was one of many directives that came to light with the findings of the Church Commission. See, e.g., John Kifner, "FBI Sought Doom of Panther Party," *New York Times,* May 9, 1976.
3. The coloring book is described in numerous sources, but see esp. Marshall "Eddie" Conway and Dominque Stevenson, *Marshall Law: The Life & Times of a Balti-*

more Black Panther (Oakland, CA: AK Press, 2011), 55–56. Also visit the Black Panther Party FBI File at the New York Public Library, http://archives.nypl.org/scm/20543.

4. Some fine general sources describing effects of COINTELPRO and general government interference in the Black Panther Party are Robyn C. Spencer, *The Revolution Has Come: Black Power, Gender, and the Black Panther Party in Oakland* (Durham, NC: Duke University Press, 2016), and Joshua Bloom and Waldo E. Martin, Jr., *Black Against Empire: The History and Politics of the Black Panther Party* (Berkeley: University of California Press, 2013). Also see online The Freedom Archives, site: https://freedomarchives.org.

5. Hampton's popularity had much to do with his ability to unite racial communities: "[W]hen I talk about the masses, I'm talking about the white masses, I'm talking about the Black masses, and the Brown masses, and the yellow masses, too. . . . [S]ome people say you fight fire best with fire, but we say you put fire out best with water. We say you don't fight racism with racism. We're gonna fight racism with solidarity. We say you don't fight capitalism with no Black capitalism; you

fight capitalism with socialism." ("Power Anywhere Where There's People," 1969 speech at Olivet Church, https://www.historyisaweapon.com/defcon1/fhampton speech.html. Also see, e.g., Jeffrey Haas, *The Assassination of Fred Hampton: How the FBI and the Chicago Police Murdered a Black Panther* (Chicago, Chicago Review Press, 2011).

6. Alprentice "Bunchy" Carter, 26, founder of the Southern California BPP chapter, and John Huggins, 23, Los Angeles Panther leader: Both shot to death in a UCLA classroom by rival group set up by FBI, January 17, 1969.

7. Des Moines bombing: In April 1969, the Black Panther Party headquarters in Des Moines, Iowa, was bombed. Police arrived on the scene about thirty seconds later and began confiscating documents. See Bloom and Martin, *Black Against Empire: The History and Politics of the Black Panther Party,* 373.

8. "People's Health Leader Expresses Hope to Emerge from Bankruptcy," Pamela Wood, *Baltimore Sun,* February 11, 2015.

9. May 1969 FBI memo from J. Edgar Hoover: "The BCP (Breakfast for Children Program) promotes at least tacit support for the Black Panther Party among

naive individuals and, what is more distressing, it provides the BPP with a ready audience composed of highly impressionable youths. Consequently, the BCP represents the best and most influential activity going for the BPP and, as such, is potentially the greatest threat to efforts by authorities . . . to neutralize the BPP and destroy what it stands for." Cited in numerous sources, e.g., Andrea King Collier, "The Black Panthers: Revolutionaries, Free Breakfast Pioneers," *National Geographic,* November 4, 2015.

Chapter 8: Give Us That Man!

1. Eugene Leroy Anderson, 20, was a suspected informer, whose tortured body was found in Baltimore's Leakin Park, October 1969. See, e.g., "Prosecutor Says New York Lawyer Ordered the Slaying of Panther," *New York Times,* June 17, 1971.
2. Panther leaders Bobby Seale and Ericka Huggins were accused of orchestrating the killing of alleged police informant Alex Rackley in New Haven, Connecticut. After over a year of a "media circus" and trial, Seale and Huggins were released when the jury failed to reach a verdict. See Yohuru Williams, *Black Politics/White Power: Civil*

Rights, Black Power, and the Black Panthers in New Haven (Hoboken, NJ: Wiley-Blackwell, 2000).

3. See, e.g., Jeff Gottlieb and Jeff Cohen, "Was Fred Hampton Executed?" *Nation,* December 25, 1976.

4. For more on the NSA and surveillance, see any number of sources, including Katelyn Epsley-Jones and Christina Frenzel, PBS Frontline, *Spying on the Home Front,* "The Church Committee Hearings and the FISA Court," May 2007, https://www.pbs.org/wgbh/pages/frontline/home front/preemption/churchfisa.html.

Chapter 9: We're Cool, and Fuck What They Say

1. At first, prosecutors charged Arthur Turco, a white, radical lawyer, with Anderson's torture and murder. When those charges didn't stick, various Baltimore BPP members were charged. Eventually, a high-school student, Irving [Ochiki Lumumba] Young, was convicted of the murder. But in 1975, Young, swearing his innocence, took a lie detector test, passed, and was pardoned that Christmas. In a 2006 interview, he maintained he never met Eugene Anderson. See Christina

Royster-Hemby, "Fighting the Power," *Baltimore City Paper,* February 8, 2006.

2. In 1990, Peter Ward, a prosecuting attorney, reflected on the case, "The greatest difficulty in the State's case was that we didn't have any direct evidence and we didn't have a direct eyewitness." Joy James, ed., *Warfare in the American Homeland: Policing and Prison in a Penal Democracy* (Durham, NC: Duke University Press, 2007), 97.

3. Judge Harris praised McAllister's lawyering: *Baltimore Afro American Newspaper,* March 6, 1971, 1. For other summaries of Eddie's case, see *Warfare in the American Homeland,* Joy James, ed., chapter 5, 96–97; Gregory Kane, "Supporters of a Pardon Think Lie Sent Man to Prison," *Baltimore Sun,* April 8, 2001; Kane, "City Council Should Check the Facts on Officer's Killer," *Baltimore Sun,* April 4, 2001; *Conway v. State,* 15 Md. App. 198 (Md. Ct. Spec. App. 1972).

4. Conway, *Marshall Law,* 43.

5. Eddie, speaking about a "system overload": (1) "Stuff down in New Orleans": In November 1970, 250 fifty police officers attempted to evict Panther members from a public housing project, where the Party had established tutoring and chil-

dren's food programs. Twelve Panther members were later acquitted of attempted murder charges incurred while resisting eviction, "1971: Black Panthers Acquitted after Tangle with New Orleans Police," *The Times-Picayune,* December 15, 2011. (2) Geronimo Ji Jaga Pratt: Los Angeles Panther leader, was framed by the FBI for the murder of Caroline Olsen, an elementary school teacher. After twenty-seven years in prison, Pratt's conviction was vacated after evidence emerged showing that the FBI, through its wiretaps, knew Pratt was in another city at the time of the murder. Released in 1997, Pratt died of a heart attack in Tanzania in 2011. Douglas Martin, "Elmer G. Pratt, Jailed Panther Leader, Dies at 63," *New York Times,* June 3, 2011. Several books include Pratt's story, notably, Jack Olsen, *Last Man Standing: The Tragedy and Triumph of Geronimo Pratt* (New York: 2011). (3) Huey Newton (with Bobby Seale, David Hilliard, and Eldridge Cleaver among others) in Oakland, California, is a recognized founder of the Black Panther Party. He spent time in prison, convicted of voluntary manslaughter in the 1967 killing of a police officer. The conviction was later reversed on appeal and after two subsequent mistrials, the state declined to pursue the case. See various newspaper, journal articles, Panther histories. Newton's autobiography is *Revolutionary Suicide* (New York: Random House, 1973).

Chapter 10: Life Plus Thirty Years

1. Conway, *Marshall Law,* 176.
2. Eddie describes the collective as based on the Panther model of Self-Defense, particularly to confront beatings by guards of imprisoned Black men, usually those sent for further punishment in "the hole." Eddie had his shoulder and jaw broken by a guard "goon squad" in retaliation for the collective's protest of one particularly harsh beating. The collective also promoted political education and communication skills. "Soon, the entire lockup area was our own university and training center." See Conway, *Marshall Law,* 121–29.
3. See, e.g., Dan Berger, *Captive Nation: Black Prison Organizing in the Civil Rights Era* (Chapel Hill: University of North Carolina Press, 2014), 91–176.
4. See Conway, *Marshall Law,* 83–92.
5. Taking photos at a prison visit can be a surreal experience. Usually, the visitor pays for them upfront, buying tickets at a

vending machine or handing some dollar bills to a guard, who then authorizes a designated prisoner to snap with an Instamatic a shot of you and the person you're visiting. You're usually posed in front of a totally out-of-context backdrop, such as a sandy beach or idyllic forest scene, as if you were on vacation. This skewed reality becomes a record of what you mean to one another.

6. A program started in 1963 by former prisoner Bill Sands, who wrote a book called *The Seventh Step* (Wise, VA: Napoleon Hill Foundation, 2013). Made up of people in and outside prison, seeking to reduce recidivism and build safer communities, the Seven Steps spread across the United States, and still exists, though its numbers have decreased. Site: http://www.7thstep.org/blog/?page_id=2.

7. Formed in 1980, the National Black Independent Political Party was an effort to address growing concerns of African American communities and break out of the two-party system. See Warren Neal Holmes, *The National Black Independent Political Party: Political Insurgency or Ideological Convergence? (Studies in African American History and Culture)* (New York: Routledge, 1999); also Conway, *Marshall*

Law, 155–56.

8. Famous Amos: See Conway, *Marshall Law,* "Civic Awareness and Famous Amos," 153–57.

9. US soldiers stationed at Abu Ghraib went to work in prisons in more than one state. See, e.g., Seymour Hersh, "Torture at Abu Ghraib," *The New Yorker,* April 30, 2004; Ariel Sabar, "Accused of Abuse, Soldier Goes from Patriot to Pariah," *Baltimore Sun,* May 9, 2004, Ariel Sabar, Gus Sentementes, Jeff Barker, "Families of the 372nd Tormented by Stories of POW Abuses in Iraq," *Baltimore Sun,* April 30, 2004.

10. 600,000 released: Actually, the US Justice Department says numbers of people released from prison yearly is higher, "More than 650,000 ex-offenders are released from prison every year, and studies show that approximately two-thirds will likely be rearrested within three years of release." US Department of Justice, site: https://www.justice.gov/archive/fbci/progmenu_reentry.html.

11. See, Christina Jedra, "New Policy Bans First Hugs and Kisses on Visits to Maryland State Prisons," *Capital Gazette,* December 12, 2015.

12. "Report Shows African Americans Lost

Half Their Wealth Due to Housing Crisis and Unemployment," National Low-Income Housing Coalition, August 30, 2013, site: https://nlihc.org/resource/report-shows-AfricanAmericans-lost-half-their-wealth-due-housing-crisis-and-unemployment. Among many other sources.

Chapter 11: Paul and Eddie and Then the World

1. Jackie Powell's death: Christine Royster-Hemby, "Fighting the Power," *Baltimore City Paper,* February 8, 2006.
2. While working here, Paul also co-edited (with Elinor Des Verney Sinnette and Thomas C. Battle) *Black Bibliophiles and Collectors: Preservers of Black History* (Howard University Press, 1990).
3. One person [Wendell Beard] rearrested: Tim Prudente, "Nonprofit Points to Maryland Unger Cases as Proof Oldest Prisoners Should Be Set Free," *Baltimore Sun,* November 15, 2018; Kevin Rector, "Convicted Baltimore Murderer, Released from Life Sentence, Is Arrested with Guns, Fentanyl, Police Say," *Baltimore Sun,* December 8, 2017.

Chapter 12: Are You Still a Revolutionary?

1. Jasmine Abdullah Richards, a founder of the Pasadena Black Lives Matter chapter, became the first Black person convicted under California's anti-lynching law for pulling a woman away from a police arrest on August 29, 2015.
2. This seems to be Allen Bullock who, at eighteen, smashed a traffic cone through a car window, protesting Freddie Gray's murder in 2015 (discovered through activist channels). Bullock was given twelve years, but was later released on probation. In July 2017, because of an address change, he missed court appearances and was resentenced to four years. At the time of this writing, he is in Maryland's Eastern Correctional Institution. See also, Jessica Anderson, "Teen Who Smashed Traffic Cone through Car Window during 2015 Unrest Returns to Prison for Violating Probation," *Baltimore Sun,* July 13, 2017.
3. The goals and work of organizations like Black Lives Matter and Movement for Black Lives constantly evolve and develop. Paul's and Eddie's views can be amplified — or contradicted — by innumerable people involved in these organizations. See, e.g., Barbara Ransby, *Making All Black*

Lives Matter: Reimagining Freedom in the Twenty-First Century (Oakland: University of California Press, 2018).

4. See, e.g., Adam Weinstein, "Inside the Military-Police Center that Spies on Baltimore's Rioters," *Gawker,* May 1, 2015, site: http://phasezero.gawker.com/inside-the-military-police-center-that-spies-on-baltimo-1700670585.

5. Third Popular Uprising of Youth, or 3° Acampamento Nacional do Levante Popular da Juventude, held in Brazil, 2016. An outgrowth of Brazil's Landless Rural Workers' Movement, or MST, the Popular Uprising of Youth seems to have started around 2007 as a result of an initiative encouraging social movements to connect rural and urban youth.

6. Paul Coates with host Peter Slen, "Tour of Black Classic Press," CSPAN, February 20, 2018, site: https://www.c-span.org/video/?441322-2/tour-black-classic-press.

Chapter 13: That Next Chapter: A Retrospective

1. Late in 2016, the Black Panther Party for Self-Defense held reunions in cities across the United States. Paul and Eddie went to the Black Panther Party Commemoration

and Conference in Oakland. See, e.g., lo-cal community radio notice, site: https://kpfa.org/event/black-panther-party-50th-anniversary/.

2. In 1948, the United Nations defined genocide as any act "committed with intent to destroy, in whole or in part, a national, ethnical, racial or religious group, as such: killing members of the group; causing serious bodily or mental harm to members of the group; deliber-ately inflicting on the group conditions of life calculated to bring about its physical destruction in whole or in part; imposing measures intended to prevent births within the group; [and] forcibly transferring children of the group to another group." This definition was crucial for African American movements in defining their historical and current conditions in the United States. See, W. E. B. DuBois, *We Charge Genocide: The Historic Petition to the United Nations for Relief from a Crime of the United States Government Against the Negro People* (New York: Civil Rights Congress, 1st ed., 1951).

Afterword: Inside Eddie Conway's Story Is So Much Black History

1. Bundy Family: cattle ranchers notorious for their long conflict with the US Bureau of Land Management over rights to graze cattle on federal land. Their resistance grew to armed militias in standoffs with federal agents. The most well known was in January 2016, when the Bundys and their supporters took over a wildlife refuge in Oregon and occupied it for forty-one days. One rancher was killed, but most defendants were acquitted or given probation, and no Bundy supporter served serious jail time.

2. Ta-Nehisi Coates, "The Case for Reparations," *The Atlantic,* June 2014, site: https://www.theatlantic.com/magazine/archive/2014/06/the-case-for-reparations/361631/.

3. Henry Louis Gates, Jr., "Author Ta-Nehisi Coates, activist Janet Mock, and filmmaker Ava DuVernay, learn new details about their ancestors," *Finding Your Roots,* PBS, October 24, 2017." (Although Gates doesn't bring up the FBI's targeting Paul Coates in this TV segment [site: https://www.youtube.com/watch?v=XTsr0h3tdXk], a reference to this letter does occur in Ta-Nehisi Coates, "My President

Was Black," *We Were Eight Years in Power: An American Tragedy* [New York: One World, 2017]).

4. Coates, "Notes from the Eighth Year," *We Were Eight Years in Power,* 291. "I don't ever want to forget that resistance must be its own reward, since resistance, at least within the lifespan of the resistors, almost always fails."

5. Coates, chapter 1, "There Lived a Little Boy Who Was Misled," *The Beautiful Struggle: A Father, Two Sons, and an Unlikely Road to Manhood* (New York: Spiegel & Grau, 2009), 8. (See also, "In My Male Stuff," chapter 11 in this book.)

The Black Panther Party Ten Point Program

1. Thanks to the exhaustive research of Joshua Bloom and Waldo E. Martin Jr., who wrote *Black Against Empire.*